# asian martial arts

## constructive thoughts & practical applications

Edited by Michael A. DeMarco, M.A.

presented by the
*Journal of Asian Martial Arts*

Via Media Publishing
Santa Fe, NM

**Disclaimer**
Please note that the authors and publisher of this book are not responsible in any manner whatsoever for any injury that may result from practicing the techniques and/or following the instructions given within, since the physical activities described herein may be too strenuous in nature for some readers to engage in safely, it is essential that a physician be consulted prior to training.

**All Rights Reserved**
No part of this publication, including illustrations, may be reproduced or utilized in any form or by any means, electronic or mechanical, including photocopying, recording, or by any information storage and retrieval system (beyond that copying permitted by Sections 107 and 108 of the U.S. Copyright Law and except by reviewers for the public press), without written permission from Via Media Publishing Company. **Warning:** Any unauthorized act in relation to a copyright work may result in both a civil clam for damages and criminal prosecution.

**Printed in the United States of America**
The paper in this book meets the guidelines for permanence and durability of the Committee on Production Guidelines for Book Longevity of the Council on Library Resources.

Copyright © 2012 by
Via Media Publishing Company

Library of Congress Control Number: 2012943986
ISBN 978-1-893765-04-7 (alk. paper)
ISBN 978-1-893765-96-2 (second edition 2022)

First published in 2012 by
Via Media Publishing Company
941 Calle Mejia #822
Santa Fe, NM 87501 USA
Tel: 1-505-983-1919 • E-mail: contact@viamediapublishing.com

Book and cover design by
Via Media Publishing Company.

Cover illustration by
Chang Jungshan (張榕柵) and Jungshan Inc.

www.journalofasianmartialarts.com

**Dedication**
This book is dedicated to
the memory of my parents,
Ralph DeMarco and
Janet Balchunas DeMarco.

# contents

vi     **Author Bionotes**

xiv    **Preface**
        Michael DeMarco, M.A.

## Constructive Thoughts

2      Writing Sword: Twenty Years of Thought, Action, and Inspiration from the *Journal of Asian Martial Arts*
        John J. Donohue, Ph.D.

10     Martial Arts History from One Era to the Next
        Robert Dohrenwend, Ph.D.

14     Fists and Phantoms: Martial Arts and Media
        James Grady, B.A.

18     An Optimal Elixir:
        Blending Spiritual, Healing, and Combative Components
        Michael Maliszewski, Ph.D.

24     Academic Research into Chinese Martial Arts:
        Problems and Perspectives
        Kai Filipiak, Ph.D.

28     Nicks and Cuts: Continuing Endeavors in Japanese Budo
        Dave Lowry, B.A.

32     The Ongoing Construction
        Linking Taekwondo Practice with Academic Research
        Willy Pieter, Ph.D.

36     The Whole Shebang Concerning Southeast Asian Martial Arts
        Kirstin Pauka, Ph.D.

# Practical Applications

| | | |
|---|---|---|
| 40 | Classical Taekwondo | Manuel Adrogué, M.A., J.D. |
| 44 | Iaido and Judo | Peter Boylan, M.A. |
| 48 | Sinmoo Hapkido | Sean Bradley, N.D., E.A.M.P. |
| 52 | Clinch Fighting, Chinese Style | Jake Burroughs |
| 58 | Wing Chun | Joyotpaul Chaudhuri, Ph.D. |
| 62 | Kuntao, Silat | Philip H. J. Davies, Ph.D. |
| 66 | Chen Taijiquan | David Gaffney, B.A. |
| 70 | Ryukyu Kenpo and Small Circle Jujitsu | Will Higginbotham, B.A. |
| 74 | Baguazhang | Hong Tsehan |
| 78 | Wei Kuen Do | Adam James |
| 82 | Small Circle Jujitsu | Leon Jay |
| 86 | Kodokan Judo | Llyr Jones, Ph.D. |
| 90 | Muso Shinden-ryu Iaido | Deborah Klens-Bigman, Ph.D. |
| 94 | Sambo | Stephen Koepfer, M.A., L.M.T. |
| 98 | Goju-ryu Karate | Marvin Labbate |
| 102 | Mixed Martial Arts | Tim Lajcik, B.A. |
| 106 | Zheng-Style Taijiquan | Russ Mason, M.A. |
| 110 | Ryukyu Kobudo Shinkokai | Mario McKenna, M.Sc. |
| 114 | Mantis Boxing | Ilya Profatilov, M.A. |
| 118 | Combat Systema | Kevin Secours, B.Ed. |
| 124 | Modern Arnis | Ken Smith |
| 128 | Jujutsu and Judo | Nicklaus Suino, J.D. |
| 132 | Niten Ichi-ryu and Shinto-ryu | Kim Taylor, M.Sc. |
| 136 | Ving Tsun Double Knives | Jeff Webb |
| 140 | Bajiquan | Tony Yang |
| 144 | Goshin Jutsu and Washin-ryu | Linda Yiannakis, M.S. |
| 148 | Taiji Spear | Yun Zhang, M.A. |

# Afterword

154 The Secrets of an Asian Martial Arts Publisher
*Michael DeMarco, M.A.*

168 Materials for Research and Practice
180 Index

# author bionotes

**Manuel E. Adrogué, M.A., J.D.,** has been practicing Taekwondo since 1983. In 2009 he received his sixth-degree from Mr. Han Chang Kim, the father of Taekwondo in Argentina. A student of Pedro Florindo, Adrogué received lessons from many of the twentieth century's Korean martial arts luminaries. He has published more than forty articles in Spanish and English focusing on martial art history and technique. He is a lawyer (Universidad de Buenos Aires, 1991) with a master's degree in business law (Universidad Austral, 1995). He is married with four children. ‣ www.taekwon.com.ar

**Peter Boylan, M.A.,** has a master's degree in comparative religions, specializing in the religious traditions of Japan. His master's thesis was titled "Aikido as Spiritual Practice in the United States." He spent six years living and training in Japan. He has trained in Japanese martial arts for twenty-six years. He trains in Kodokan judo, Shinto Hatakage-ryu Iai Heiho, and Shinto Muso-ryu. For nearly fifteen years Boylan has run Mugendo Budogu, LLC, providing very high-quality martial art products from Japan, including custom-made items. ‣ www.budogu.com

**Sean Bradley, N.D., E.A.M.P.,** is a seventh-degree black belt in Sinmoo Hapkido under its founder, Dojunim Ji Han-Jae. He has served as Ji's personal assistant for the last fifteen years and accompanies him around the world, teaching seminars. He is a naturopathic physician and East Asian-medicine practitioner who runs a private practice in Seattle, Washington. He sees patients and teaches classes daily while continuing his studies in Asian languages and literature at the University of Washington. ‣ www.washingtonhapkido.com

**Jake Burroughs** has been a student of Tim Cartmell and Hu Xilin for over a decade. Jake splits his time teaching and training, as well as running his blog, "The Ground Never Misses." Jake is also a sponsored competitive athlete under 1914 Kimonos. Combining twenty years of martial arts experience, Jake hopes to bridge the gap between reality and fantasy when approaching the traditional martial arts. Principles of physics and biomechanics govern all humans regardless of "style" or origin of system. ‣ www.threeharmonies.com

**Chang Jungshan** (張榕柵) **B.A.,** received her degree from the Chinese Culture University in Taipei. She works full-time with a technology company in Taipei, but greatly enjoys working as a freelance artist under the name of JungShan Ink. Largely self-taught, she draws inspiration from traditional Chinese brush techniques and magically merges it with Western styles using contemporary digital techniques. Jungshan's creativity and sensitivity produce captivating images that are full of life, as seen in her depiction of warriors in motion.
‣ http://jung-shan.blogspot.com

**Joyotpaul "Joy" Chaudhuri, Ph.D.**, attended Calcutta University (I. Sc., science diploma). He practiced Indian martial arts and Western boxing. He received his Ph.D. from Oklahoma University. He is a professor emeritus at Arizona State University, where he taught political philosophy and comparative politics. He is an ex-associate dean for academic affairs of the College of Liberal Arts and Sciences. He has studied several different Asian martial arts but his central style since 1976 has been Wing Chun gongfu.
‣ www.tempewingchun.com

**Philip H. J. Davies, Ph.D.**, is known primarily as a scholar on intelligence and security issues, although he has published substantially on kuntao and its relationship to the Indo-Malay martial arts. He is director of the Brunel University Centre for Intelligence and Security Studies. He has just published the two-volume *Intelligence and Government in Britain and the United States: A Comparative Approach* (Praeger Security International, 2012) and was one of the authors of the current British Joint Intelligence Doctrine. ‣ www.brunel.ac.uk/bciss

**Michael DeMarco, M.A.**, received his degree from Seton Hall University's Asian Studies Department. In 1964 he began studies of Indonesian kuntao-silat. Since 1973 he has focused on Taijiquan: Yang style, Xiong Yanghe lineage; Chen style, Du Yuze lineage. He founded Via Media Publishing Company in 1991, producing the *Journal of Asian Martial Arts* and books. He presented a number of academic papers at international conferences, published nearly seventy-five articles, and has been interviewed for documentaries appearing on the Discovery Channel, Arts & Entertainment, and the History Channel. He teaches Taiji in Santa Fe, New Mexico.

**Robert E. Dohrenwend, Ph.D.**, received his degree from Syracuse University in micrometeorology. He has been an enthusiastic hunter with the traditional longbow for over a quarter of a century, and his martial arts experiences range from the Hungarian saber to Okinawan and Japanese karate and Korean Taekwondo. Dr. Dohrenwend served as an associate editor for the *Journal of Asian Martial Arts*, providing excellent editorial skills and contributing some of the highest-quality articles on topics such as the sai, sling, spear, and walking stick. "Dangerous Animals and the Asian Martial Arts" was in Vol. 19 No. 1.

**John J. Donohue, Ph.D.**, received his degree in anthropology from the State University of New York at Stony Brook. His doctoral dissertation on the cultural aspects of the Japanese martial arts formed the basis for his first book, *The Forge of the Spirit*. He is the author of both nonfiction books as well as many articles on the martial arts. Dr. Donohue is a pioneer in a new genre of martial art thrillers, with a series starting with *Sensei* (Onyx, 2004), followed by *Deshi* (Onyx, 2006), *Tengu* (YMAA, 2008), and *Kage* (YMAA, 2011). He has black belt ranks in both karatedo and kendo.
‣ www.johndonohue.net

# author bionotes

**Kai Filipiak, Ph.D.,** is an associate professor of Chinese Studies at Leipzig University in Germany. He is the author of two superb books in German that deal with Chinese martial traditions: *Die Chinesische Kampfkunst: Spiegel und Element Traditioneller Chinesischer Kultur* (*Chinese Fighting Arts: Mirror and Element of Traditional Chinese Culture*, Leipzig University, 2001) and *Krieg, Staat und Militär in der Ming-Zeit* (*War, State and Military in Ming Times*, Harrassowitz, 2008).

**David Gaffney, B.A.,** received his degree in leisure and human communication from Manchester University, England. He has been training in the Asian martial arts since 1980 and received an instructor's certificate from the Chenjiagou Taijiquan School. He holds a sixth-degree grade with the Chinese Wushu Association. He won a gold medal at the 1997 International Atlantic Cup. Mr. Gaffney has made numerous trips to train with some of the leading figures of Chen Taijiquan, including Chen Xiaowang and Chen Xiaoxing. With Davidine Siaw-Voon Sim he is the co-author of *The Essence of Taijiquan* (Blurb Books). ‣ www.chentaijigb.co.uk

**James Grady, B.A.,** studied a variety of martial arts, but focuses on Taiji's Yang short form, Zheng Manqing style. His first Taiji teacher was Robert W. Smith. Grady's degree is from the University of Montana. He's a fiction author best known for his novel *Six Days of the Condor* (which inspired the Robert Redford film). His most recent novel is *Mad Dogs*, in which five former CIA operatives, now living in a government-run, top-secret insane asylum in Maine, break out after their psychiatrist is murdered. He's a recipient of numerous literary awards.
‣ www.jamesgrady.net

**Will Higginbotham** studied a variety of martial art styles, but by the mid-1980s, he had become one of the many martial artists to train directly under four affiliated headmasters: George Dillman (Ryukyu Kempo), Wally Jay (Small Circle Jujitsu), Remy Presas (Modern Arnis), and Leo Fong (Wei Kuen Do). Higginbotham presently holds a ninth-degree rank in Ryukyu Kempo and a fifth-degree rank in Small Circle Jujitsu.
‣ www.theryukyudojo.com

**Hong Tsehan**（洪澤漢）is the second son of Master Hong Yixiang（洪懿祥, 1920–1993). He has been training in the Yizong Tangshoudao lineage（易宗唐手道）of his father for close to fifty years. He has had a varied career, directing award-winning television shows, as an executive in advertising and media, as deputy general manager of the Taipei Sheraton Hotel managing an acclaimed renovation of the property, and presently as the vice president in a securities brokerage firm. He resides in Taiwan with his wife and two sons.

**Adam James** is the designated successor of Leo Fong, the founder and headmaster of the art of Wei Kuen Do. In addition to his training with Fong, Mr. James has experience in a wide variety of other martial arts, including Michael Dela Vega's Okinawan Kempo. Mr. James is the founder of Rainbow Warrior Martial Arts, and also has a successful career as an actor and a writer, appearing in such films as *Under Siege* with Steven Seagal and *Steal Big/Steal Little* with Andy Garcia.
‣ www.rainbowwarriormartialarts.com

**Leon Jay** is the son of Grandmaster Wally Jay, the founder and first generation headmaster of the art of Small Circle Jujitsu. Leon Jay has been the headmaster of the Small Circle system since his father retired in 2002. In addition to his rank in the Small Circle system, Grandmaster Jay holds senior dan ranks in several other styles, including Kodenkan Jujitsu.
‣ www.smallcirclejujitsu.com

**Llyr Jones, Ph.D.**, received his degree from the University of Southampton and is an independent scholar, multi-published author, and associate editor of the *Journal of Asian Martial Arts*. A former international-level judo competitor, he has studied judo for extended periods in Japan and France. He is an enthusiastic proponent of traditional, well-rounded judo as envisioned by Kano Jigoro, and prefers to teach judo without limiting himself to any specific group or organization. Dr. Jones' current research interests are focused on judo's historical aspects and katas.

**Deborah Klens-Bigman, Ph.D.**, has studied Muso Shinden-ryu iaido for over twenty-six years. Her interest in other traditional Japanese martial arts includes short staff (*jodo*), halberd (*naginatado*), archery (*kyudo*), and other sword styles. She holds a Ph.D. from New York University's Department of Performance Studies and has published numerous articles in both paper and online journals, including the *Asian Theatre Journal*, and the *Journal of Asian Martial Arts*. She has also made contributions to compilations, including *The Encyclopedia of Women in Sport*, and co-authored *Kyudo: The Way of the Bow*. ‣ www.dklens-bigman.com

**Stephen Koepfer** is head coach of New York Combat Sambo and president of the American Sambo Association. He has coached his team to wins in Sambo, grappling, Sanshou, Muay Thai, and MMA, and was a coach at the 2008 FIAS World Sambo Championships. He was awarded Master of Sport of Russia in 2009. Stephen is widely published and has served as an advisor for *Human Weapon* and *Dhani Tackles the Globe*, and is producer of the acclaimed documentary *New York Mixed Martial Arts*. He earned his master's degree in creative arts therapy from Hosftra University and is a licensed massage therapist. ‣ www.nycombatsambo.com

# author bionotes

**Marvin Labbate** is an eighth-degree black belt in Okinawan Goju-ryu and a sixth-degree in Okinawan Ryukonkai Kobudo. He has studied karate for over forty-five years and is the international director for the Okinawan Seibukai Association. Mr. Labbate is the director of CNY Karate, founded in 1963, which is the oldest karate school in upstate New York. Labbate published five articles in the *Journal of Asian Martial Arts*, the most recent in Volume 20 Number 1, "Attention, Sit, Meditate, Bow, Ready Position: Ritualized Dojo Pattern or Character Training?"
‣ www.cnykarate.com

**T. G. LaFredo, B.S.**, holds degrees in English and criminology and is currently completing work on an M.F.A. in creative writing. A former police officer, he is a graduate of the Police Training Institute at the University of Illinois. He began his martial studies in 1998. Mr. LaFredo served as copy editor of the *Journal of Asian Martial Arts* from December 2009 through the final issue and continues with Via Media Publishing's other endeavors.
‣ http://tglafredo.com

**Tim Lajcik, B.A.**, earned his degree in sociology at the University of California–Davis, where he also served as head wrestling coach and is an inductee in the university's Athletics Hall of Fame. A collegiate All-American in wrestling and football, Tim went on to capture a freestyle wrestling national championship, win a regional Golden Gloves amateur boxing championship, and compete as a professional mixed martial arts fighter in the Ultimate Fighting Championships. He currently works as an actor and stunt performer, and teaches fighting and wrestling seminars throughout the United States and abroad. ‣ www.TimLajcik.net

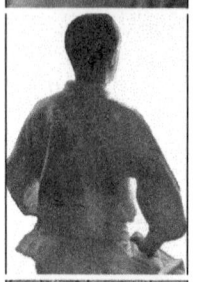

**David Lowry, B.S.**, has been involved in the classical and modern Japanese martial disciplines since 1968, focusing on Yagu Shinkage-ryu, Shindo Muso-ryu, and Aikido. He is the author of eight books on Japan's martial culture, including *Autumn Lightning: The Education of an American Samurai* (Shambhala, 2001), *The Essence of Budo: A Practitioner's Guide to Understanding the Japanese Martial Ways* (Shambhala, 2010), and *Clouds in the West: Lessons from the Martial Arts of Japan* (Lyons Press, 2004). Lowry has a baccalaureate in English from Southwest Missouri State University.

**Michael Maliszewski, Ph.D.**, is a psychologist affiliated with Massachusetts General Hospital and Harvard Medical School. He received his Ph.D. from the University of Chicago. He has instructor rankings in Kobojutsu/tedo, Modified Wing Chun, and Cabales Serrada Escrima and most recently with Brazilian Jiujitsu and Systema. Dr. Maliszewski also has advanced training and experience in several systems of meditation. His current research involves investigating models to accelerate healing in patients though modification of traditional healing systems and completing a long-overdue book on human sexuality.

**Russ Mason, M.A., TESL**, received his degree from Oklahoma State University, teaches language and culture at the University of Delaware, and has taught Taijiquan for the University of Delaware's College of Health and Nursing Science and Confucius Institute. Mason served on the *Journal of Asian Martial Arts* editorial staff from 2005 to 2012. With a background in yoga and judo in the 1960s, he began training in Yang-style Taijiquan in the 1970s in the lineage of Professor Zheng Manqing, initially with Dr. B. A. Fusaro. His primary teachers were Robert W. Smith (U.S.) and Liu Xiheng (Taiwan).

**Mario McKenna, M.Sc.**, began his karate training in Gohakukai under Yoshitaka Kinjo in 1984 in Lethbridge, Alberta. He resided in Japan from 1994 to 2002, where he studied Ryukyu Kobudo under Minowa Katsuhiko and Yoshimura Hiroshi, and Tou'on-ryu Karatedo under Kanzaki Shigekazu and Ikeda Hidenori. He holds a master of science degree in physical education from the University of Saskatchewan, and a master of health administration degree from the University of British Columbia.
‣ www.kowakan.com

**Kirstin Pauka, Ph.D.**, is a professor in the Department of Theatre and Dance at the University of Hawai'i at Manoa. She has served as an associate editor for the *Journal of Asian Martial Arts*, and authored four articles dealing with Indonesian martial arts. Other works include *Theater & Martial Arts in West Sumatra: Randai & Silek of the Minangkabau* (Ohio University Press, 1999) and, on CD-ROM, *Randai: Folk Theater, Dance, and Martial Arts of West Sumatra* (University of Michigan Press, 2002). Dr. Pauka practices Japanese taiko drumming and trains in Aikido, Taekwondo, and silek. ‣ www.ohioswallow.com/author/Kirstin+Pauka

**Willy Pieter, Ph.D.**, received his doctorate in physical education from the University of Oregon in Eugene. He is currently a professor in the Department of Taekwondo at Keimyung University in Daegu, Korea. He initiated the first multidisciplinary scientific research project on elite adult Taekwondo athletes at the U.S. Olympic Training Center in Colorado Springs. Additionally, Dr. Pieter published a number of articles with the *Journal of Asian Martial Arts*, and he also served as an associate editor. He is coauthor of *Scientific Coaching for Olympic Taekwondo* (Meyer and Meyer, 2000).

**Ilya Profatilov, M.A.**, has been the leading researcher in Mantis Boxing for the last twenty years. He has studied extensively with the venerable masters Ma Hanqing, Wang Yuanqian, Lin Tangfang, and many others. Mr. Profatilov is currently compiling all of his research into a book which he expects to publish by next summer. He holds a master's degree in Chinese history and religions from Moscow State University and studied in a doctoral program at Indiana University of Bloomington.
‣ www.mantiskungfuacademy.com

# author bionotes

**Kevin Secours, B.Ed.,** is a sixth-degree black belt in Goshinbudo, a third-dan in Modern Kempo Jujitsu, a first-dan in Akai-ryu Jujutsu and a full instructor in Five Animal Shaolin Boxing. The director of training for the Quebec Tactical Training Center, he is a fully certified defensive tactics instructor and works actively in personal protection. Also one of the most renowned experts in Russian Systema in North America, he is the founder of the International Combat Systema Association, a non-profit organization dedicated to the scientific refinement, integration, and preservation of the Slavic martial arts. ‣ www.combatsystema.com

**Ken Smith** began his martial training at the age of eighteen and received high rankings in a number of combative arts: sixth-dan Isshin-ryu under Jesse Gallegoes; eighth-dan Ryukyu Kempo under George Dillman. He was introduced to Modern Arnis by George Mazek and then became a direct student of Remy Presas, the founder and headmaster of the Modern Arnis style. Smith was one of only seven senior practitioners to be promoted to the level of "master of tapi-tapi," the highest level of achievement in Modern Arnis. ‣ www.modernarnisacademy.com

**Nicklaus Suino, J.D.,** holds bachelor of arts and master of fine arts degrees from the English Department at the University of Michigan, as well as a doctor of jurisprudence degree from Thomas M. Cooley Law School. He was All Tokyo Iaido Champion at his rank level for four consecutive years and has written five books—four on Japanese martial arts and one humorous guide to motivation he coauthored with Ian Gray entitled *101 Ideas to Kick Your Ass into Gear*.
‣ www.japanesemartialartscenter.com

**Kim Taylor, M.Sc.,** is an associate editor for the *Journal of Asian Martial Arts*. His degree is from the University of Guelph, where he worked for twenty-four years. He is currently the president of SDKsupplies.com and a co-owner of Proswords.com. Taylor holds teaching ranks in Aikido, iaido, and jodo; sits on the national grading panel for iaido and jodo; and is chair of the Canadian Kendo Federation Jodo section. Along the way Taylor has also practiced and taught several Japanese sword and stick koryus. An author of many instructional books and videos, he continues to edit and publish the *Electronic Journals of Martial Arts and Sciences*.

**Jeff Webb,** one of America's foremost authorities on Ving Tsun (Wing Chun), is the founder of the National Ving Tsun Organization. He is a former personal student of Leung Ting, and has trained with numerous masters and grandmasters in Europe and Asia during his twenty-seven-year career. Mr. Webb has taught well over a hundred weekend seminars throughout North America. These well-attended workshops continue to make him a popular instructor on the seminar circuit. A veteran of the U.S. Air Force, he has authored a number of articles on the martial arts and is currently working on a Ving Tsun book series. ‣ www.austinvtkungfu.com

**Tony Yang** was born in Taiwan and began training in traditional Plum Flower Praying Mantis at age six under his uncle, Wang Shujin (王樹金 1903–1981). He began to study Praying Mantis systems under Su Yuzhang and later entered into discipleship with Liu Yunqiao (劉雲樵 1909–1992). He focused on Bajiquan/Piguazhang, Bagua, Praying Mantis, and numerous traditional weapons. He also helped instruct the presidential bodyguards of Taiwan. In 1980, Tony immigrated to Canton, Ohio, and formed The Wu Tang Center for Martial Arts Association.
‣ www.wutangcenter.com

**Linda Yiannakis, M.S.**, has been practicing martial arts since 1971. She holds fourth-degree rankings in both judo and jujutsu. From the mid-1990s through 2006 she studied Kodokan judo and Takagi-ryu Kosenjo Bujutsu as a senior student of Steve Cunningham. Ms. Yiannakis currently teaches judo in Albuquerque, New Mexico, and is a senior instructor in Wa Shin-ryu jujutsu at the University of New Mexico. She is a board member of the Institute of Traditional Martial Arts at UNM. Her educational background includes an M.S. in communication development and disorders.
‣ http://unm.wsrjj.org/tradkodojudo.htm

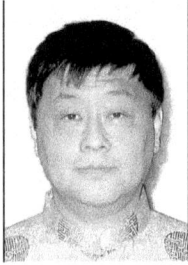

**Zhang Yun, M.S.** in computer science, is president of the Yin Cheng Gong Fa Association of North America. He learned Shaolin, Shuaijiao, and Tongbei during his teens, beginning Taiji with Luo Shuhuan in 1975. One year later he became the direct student of Wang Peisheng, the great master of Beijing, China. Under Master Wang's instruction, Zhang studied Taiji, Bagua, and Xingyi, as well as qigong. In 1983, he began teaching martial arts in China, the USA, Europe, and Australia. Zhang Yun is the author of *The Art of Chinese Swordsmanship* and *The Complete Taiji Dao*.
‣ www.ycgf.org

> "Coming together is a beginning.
> Keeping together is progress.
> Working together is success."
> ~ Henry Ford

# preface

We welcome you to imbibe a favorite bubbly drink as you read the following pages. This book represents a gathering of friends who happen to be highly qualified martial art scholars and practitioners. We have come together in celebration of the more than twenty years (1992–2012) the *Journal of Asian Martial Arts* inspired scholarship in this field to higher academic standards while encouraging all aspects of responsible practice. Each article was written specifically for this banquet, with topics representing the rich variety found in the Asian martial traditions. But what's a party without guests? As a reader, you are a special guest and part of this celebration. We hope you'll enjoy and benefit from what is to follow.

Via Media Publishing produced eighty-one issues of the *Journal of Asian Martial Arts*. This book serves as a special finale to the two decades the periodical served the field. From the book's subtitle—*Constructive Thoughts and Practical Applications*—you can see a parallel with the journal's theme of cultivating martial aspects with the civil, as symbolized in its logo.

What exactly do the Asian martial arts represent? Unfortunately, the vast majority of explanations fall far short, showing either a lack of knowledge or a strong bias in perceptions. These faults have stigmatized the field of martial arts as unworthy of serious consideration by many mainstream academicians. Fighting has been a constant in the history of human activity, so it is logical that anthropologists should deal with it as a major thread in social evolution. Professional anthropologists should have the scholarly tools to analyze and present human activities in ways that are useful to others.

We are very fortunate that Dr. John Donohue wrote the introductory article for this book. As an anthropologist and scholar/practitioner of a variety of martial arts, his article offers a concise overview of the depth and breadth of this subject. Most of us are so busy working within our own area of interest that we are not so familiar with the larger picture. Dr. Donohue's perceptions and suggestions are helpful to other scholars and practitioners.

The articles in the "Constructive Thoughts" section represent overviews within specific areas of academic interest, mainly following the geographic areas associated with the Asian martial traditions, as well as areas vital for understanding their place in society. Dr. Robert

Dohrenwend's article provides a historian's view of the field of Asian martial arts, while Filipiak, Lowry, Pieter, and Pauka cover the areas of China, Japan, Korea, and Southeast Asia, respectively.

James Grady looks at the media with an editor's eye for what is essential and superfluous for our understanding of real versus fantasy in the martial arts (as in the movie *Gladiator*, when Russell Crowe yelled: "Are you not entertained?"). In dealing with the philosophical side of Asian martial arts, Maliszewski's piece penetrates the core. A number of martial arts are directly associated with a tradition of ethical guidance, such as Aikido and Kalariplayattu. Most are not, and so may lack moral guidelines necessary for practitioners to be responsible for the lethal arts they teach and practice. The articles by Grady and Maliszewski show that martial arts don't exist in a vacuum, and that we need to look closely at how they relate to the more important aspects of life.

If the articles in the "Constructive Thoughts" section have an air of ivory tower elitism, don't worry. In defining the goals for this section, we asked each author to write from the heart, without footnotes or references. Their scholarship stands on long-established foundations. Articles here are not in the typical scholarly format. They are simply constructive thoughts shared in a personal way with fellow enthusiasts.

You may find common threads running through the articles in the "Constructive Thoughts" section. It is not a coincidence that there are similarities in areas such as history, theory, and practice. Of course, the bedrock for these articles is the combative element found in the Asian cultures represented. The fighting arts were born out of necessity as a means for survival. Therefore, twenty-seven articles in the "Practical Applications" section focus on self-defense theory and practice. The authors are well-known practitioners and highly knowledgeable in their stylistic specialization, be it a focus on grappling, striking, weaponry, or some combination. For anyone interested in Asian martial arts, these authors provide great insights into their arts by illustrating favorite techniques. They tell where they learned these techniques, recount memorable stories associated with them, and give tips for practice.

As mentioned at the start, this book is published in celebration of the

*Journal of Asian Martial Arts*' presence over the past two decades. The number of authors invited to the celebration had to be limited, so the scope of this book is not encompassing.

We hope that all readers will enjoy the material included in the "Constructive Thoughts" and "Practical Applications." All the authors delivered their own plates, filled with spicy delicacies. These are not to simply be taken and forgotten, but to be digested, absorbed, and remembered. Since this book is a finale in celebration of the *Journal of Asian Martial Arts*, I also add an article as an afterword. My goal here is to share memories and experiences as the journal's editor-in-chief that will highlight the state of martial arts scholarship and practice today, taking into account factors that foster developments as well as hinder them.

The last section of this book includes a list of materials for research and practice that readers may find helpful for further reading in their areas of interest. An index is also included for readers' convenience.

As the organizer of this compilation, I want to acknowledge all the authors who contributed. Over the years I have become familiar with each author's long involvement in the Asian martial traditions. They all deserve great respect for their unique contributions in this field. All have been involved with the *Journal of Asian Martial Arts* in some way, and I'm happy to have established many friendships with these fine scholars and practitioners.

Authors provided interesting, insightful material for this book. Reading each page should prove a smooth experience. I thank T.G. LaFredo for his masterful editing work for making this so. He handles a red pen much like a tenth-dan swordsman and Daoist healer: cutting what deserves to be removed and doctoring to bring you a healthy body of text. In addition to his knowledge and instinct for word crafting, you'll find no other person so supportive of this book project, as well as the *Journal of Asian Martial Arts*.

I'd like to personally thank all the above-mentioned people for celebrating the life of the *Journal of Asian Martial Arts* by contributing to this book, as well as all who have supported our publishing work over the years. I bear the responsibility for whatever faults you may find in this book, but hope you will find many rewards from each constructive thought and practical application.

All of us who have contributed to this book's content wish you a pleasurable read with many beneficial revisits.

# constructive thoughts

"Act like a man of thought.
Think like a man of action."

~ *Henri Louis Bergson (1859)*

*Illustration by JungShan Inc.*

# Writing Sword: Twenty Years of Thought, Action, and Inspiration from the *Journal of Asian Martial Arts*

John J. Donohue, Ph.D.

The old samurai dictum *bun bu ichi* (文武一) asserts that the ways of the pen and the sword are linked. It was a fundamental starting point for Mike DeMarco when he set out on the ambitious plan to create the premier journal to explore the richness and complexity of the Asian martial arts. Indeed, the company logo of Via Media, JAMA's parent company, is a stylized blending of sword and pen tips. That said, what many of us know in theory is often devilishly tricky to pull off in actuality. It's a tribute to Mike's devotion to the arts, his conviction regarding their importance, and his commitment to seek out the best quality material to present to the reading public, that he has been able, year after year, to do just that.

The martial arts are complex. They are physical systems of some sophistication that engage us somatically as we struggle to master technique and develop our physical skills. They involve struggle and frustration, the tug and burn of effort, the need to submit oneself to a harsh and long discipleship and expose us to the highs of elation when we get it right and the lows of disappointment when we don't. As a result, they are arts that engage us not only physically, but on emotional and psychological levels as well. The arts are also systems that have been shaped by different cultural traditions: they expose us not only to new ways of doing, but also to new ways of thinking and talking. And certainly the cultural/philosophical construct that is often associated with these arts is a major attraction for their students. For many of those pursuing the martial way, the systems, their heritage, and their philosophies hint at the possibility of expanded human potential in both physical and spiritual terms.

In an anthropological sense, the study of the Asian martial arts requires a holistic approach, one that is open to exploring any and all of the varying facets of these systems. The practical implication of this fact is that each and every attempt to write about the arts is a "yes, but …" moment. There are no definitive accounts, no final summations: there are glimpses at a facet of a jewel and, if done right, these isolated accounts encourage the reader to think and question and wonder. To rotate the jewel, turn it into the light, and explore a new facet.

This has been a real strength of the journal: it has been committed to quality thinking and writing about the Asian martial arts, but has also been open to and encouraging of varying types of articles and various types of perspectives. In the journal's pages you could explore the historical pedigree of a Taiji style, expand your repertoire of joint locks, read about martial arts as represented in literature and film, and ponder the complexity of Asian philosophy. As a result, JAMA's emphasis on quality and an expansive focus have created a publishing record of significance and depth that has been no small feat.

Anyone who has trained for any length of time in any one of the more traditional arts knows there is a right way and a wrong way to virtually anything in the training hall. The arts insist on an aesthetic of excellence, on a commitment to integrity. JAMA has sought to infuse that ethos into the works it presented for its readers.

This has been one of the more significant contributions that twenty years of JAMA has bequeathed to the serious martial arts world. Forty or so years ago, there were few easily accessible and authoritative works available to Western readers on the subject of the Asian martial arts. I think back to my own first brushes with the exotic arts of the East: rudimentary how-to manuals, cheaply produced with grainy photos and little explanatory sense of how the aspiring Shaolin monk got from the posture in picture 1 to the stance in picture 2. As time passed, the published martial arts corpus grew in breadth and quality, but these were largely (and ostensibly) instructional tomes with some cursory explorations of philosophy, history, and culture. Eventually, they grew in sophistication, and the best were handsome productions that could be pored over with some satisfaction. I know because I own a number of them. But in many ways, they were the literary equivalent of potato chips: fast food for the martial arts junkie.

What was often lacking in these works, whatever the technical merit, was a linkage to a corpus of background information that was both sophisticated and accurate. The patina of the exotic and the promise of esoteric knowledge and power, as well as the sheer historical and intellectual depth of Asian cultures, encourage a willingness to suspend the critical faculties and a tendency to accept almost any just-so story as gospel. We all "know," for instance, that Bodhidharma developed the early forms of boxing practiced by the monks of Shaolin and that these ur-forms were ancestral to contemporary empty-hand systems in Asia. But really … we also know that Bodhidharma was so incensed that his monks couldn't stay awake during meditation sessions that he cut off his eyelids and tossed them outside, where they took root and gave us the leaves for tea. So what do these just-so stories tell us? Very little in any factual sense. They are myths, stories meant to convey meanings that are important to those who hear them. As a result, they are true in some symbolic way, but not historically accurate.

What JAMA was interested in was reviving our critical faculties as we examined the Asian martial arts. The journal's editorial stance was one dedicated to creating a more nuanced and sophisticated treatment of the history, theory, and practice of the martial arts. You could certainly try to assert your favorite Bodhidharma myth was true in the journal, but you had better have some documentation to back it up. Otherwise, Mike and his associated editors would take the piece apart and insist on some grounding in fact (or at least an admission that the assertion was improvable) before it saw the light of day in print.

The journal essentially provided a place the scholarship of research on Asian martial arts could begin to develop. It was a welcome vehicle for many of us. The traditional academic world is a relatively staid place, and twenty years ago a focus on Asian martial arts was considered an unseemly dip into the murky waters of popular culture. A few of us were permitted to do so—perhaps our research directors were ultimately worn down by our obsessions. But with JAMA's support we were able to start a place where scholarly research could be shared and discussed on this endlessly fascinating topic. Historians, linguists, anthropologists, philosophers, practitioners, students of movement and human physiology, as well as others with a grounding in the foundational scholarship of Asia were able to share their relevant knowledge with JAMA's readership. This elevated the sophistication with which practicing martial artists reflected on and understood the traditions they were devoted to. But it did more than that. As a result of some of the work by scholars featured in the journal, researchers today have at their disposal a collection of fine articles on various aspects of the Asian martial arts: archeology and history, philosophy and psychology, social analysis and cultural interpretation. These works are grounded in the rigorous approaches of traditional academic research and use the tools of scholarly analysis to expand the knowledge base and understanding we have regarding the martial arts. The collected volumes of JAMA's twenty-year history constitute a treasure trove that may rightly be said to have served in part as a foundation to elevate the ways in which people think about the Asian martial arts.

A commitment to quality was also reflected in Mike's approach to prose in the journal: it had to be clear, focused, and accessible. In some ways this posed a challenge for both ends of the martial arts writing spectrum. On one hand, good practitioners do not always produce the most polished prose or even the clearest instructions. I have had senseis who admonished me to "get more front" or to "go fast but don't rush," which, in the dojo, made perfect sense. Starkly reproduced on the page, however, these little chestnuts are too cryptic and too tied to experiential learning to be useful. On the other end of the spectrum are the academics, long schooled in the use of jargon, cautious pronouncements, and theoretical evasion. As specialists, they are used to a writing style that is a type of impacted shorthand, meant to convey meaning only to fellow travelers in the discipline who have mastered the same body of knowledge and, I suspect, the secret handshake.

Mike rejected both extremes. The prose in JAMA had to take the middle way (entirely appropriate for a publication of a company called Via Media). The journal didn't dumb things down. It stressed respect for the reading audience's maturity and willingness to engage with complex topics. These readers were, after all, very often people who had invested significant time and effort in following their disciplines. They deserved the best, the most accurate, and the most comprehensive information possible. But at the same time, JAMA stressed an approach to writing that insisted on cogent clarity. The point was to make things more widely known, not to obscure matters further. In its editorial approach, JAMA worked to invite readers in, not to shut them out.

And of course, writing well is difficult. Writing well about something as complex and experiential as the martial arts is even more challenging. How, after all, do you put lightning in a bottle? The short answer is that you can't in any definitive sense. But I think a hallmark of the good writing that fills the pages of JAMA is that it provides at least a hint of the essence of things. What shines through is the energy and commitment of the writers to communicate something of value that they have discovered to like-minded readers. It may be that the Dao that can be written about is not the Dao. But many of us think the Dao is important enough to work, however imperfectly, at trying to inspire others through the written word.

So where does this lead us? How do the lessons learned, the insights generated by two decades of work, inform our work from here?

In the first place, despite the significant achievement that is embodied in JAMA's publishing record, it must be recognized that the work is not ended. We haven't exhausted the subject. There is more, much more, to do. The question is, how best to go about doing it.

First, we build on what has gone before. But this does not imply an uncritical acceptance of material. Early writing on martial arts topics was done by martial artists who were interested in informing the public, spreading the word about the arts, and, let's face it, spreading the word about themselves. They were simultaneously sources of basic (often technical) information and publicity vehicles. These works can have some value, but more often as artifacts for study than as sources for substantive research. They are what I would term "aspirational material," reflecting both the interest and hopes of the reading public as well as the career moves of the authors.

A second wave of more substantive work began to appear, often the product of a type of participant observation. The authors were often (as in my case) individuals with training in a particular academic discipline who actually practiced the martial arts and also thought them a fitting subject for academic exploration. Authors of this type provided a perspective that was simultaneously subjective and objective. By virtue of personal pursuit of training in martial arts forms, they had an intimate grounding in the dynamics of the experience, an emotional connection to that experience, and a personal conviction that the arts were worthy of study and discussion.

At the same time, they were able to bring the tools of their formal academic training to bear on the subject. This meant subjecting research and writing to the sort of rigor and methodology typically associated with academic disciplines. The collection of the works of this type in JAMA, particularly because of their documentation of primary and secondary written sources as well as their introduction of various theoretical perspectives that could be usefully applied to the subject, makes them vital starting points for any new researchers seeking to advance our scope of knowledge in the area. In short, martial arts researchers are no longer solitary and isolated iconoclasts working on an obscure topic. While the research niche we are addressing here is admittedly still a relatively narrow one, it is one with a good foundation of important work. Any writer looking to continue the agenda should acknowledge these foundations (with both their strengths and weaknesses) and use what has gone before to advance and strengthen research and writing for and about the martial arts community.

Closely linked to this is the need to maintain a high quality of research and writing. We should bring the same care and focus to our intellectual work on this topic that our sensei and shifu insist we display in our training. This means a constant stress on logical exposition and methodological rigor. It also suggests that if we are to continue the best traditions of JAMA, we should strive to constantly hone the craft of writing itself to ensure that our work is accessible and elegant at the same time.

I also believe it is vitally important for researchers and writers on martial

*Illustration by Oscar Ratti.*

arts topics to link their discussion and analysis to broader discipline-specific questions and theories. While valuable, simply documenting the mechanics, traditions, and philosophies of various Asian martial arts forms is not the ultimate purpose of our research. There is certainly a benefit in documenting what Conrad Kottak calls the wonder of human diversity, but it seems to me good scholarship is an endeavor that has a purpose beyond mere butterfly collecting. How does what we learn about the martial arts inform our understanding of human purpose, of the ways in which traditions are formed and reformed over time, the various uses they have been put to? It seems to me there are important questions in many research disciplines that could be fruitfully explored using data from martial arts research. If we are to expand the awareness of the topic and reinforce what we believe is its importance, forging this wider link with the scholarly community is vital.

At the same time, I hope we continue to be an open community, welcoming to varying perspectives and individuals with diverse backgrounds. The breadth of topics explored in twenty years of *JAMA* has demonstrated that a community of committed practitioners, thinkers and writers need not be a closed guild. This dojo is open to all those with the desire to enter and the willingness to work hard.

The sheer complexity of the martial arts also suggests to me that really strong research and writing will increasingly be done by teams of experts. As any of us who has attempted an article or book in this area knows, it is beyond the capacity of most of us as individuals to competently treat all aspects of a subject. A master technician is not necessarily a good writer. A historian is not an expert on kinesiology. An anthropologist is not a psychologist. But we have seen that individuals from all these areas and more have contributed to writing on the martial arts. Imagine how immeasurably improved our projects could be if we came together and combined our talents and insights. It is my hope that as a community of researchers, scholars, writers and practitioners coalesces in this domain, we will see an increasing emphasis on integrating multiple perspectives and skill sets to deal with the challenging and complex nature of our studies.

The growth of web-based technology also has significant potential for presenting material on martial arts topics. The herculean task of a traditional print journal such as *JAMA*, which encompasses not only content development but production and distribution, makes a difficult agenda even more so. While *JAMA* is going away, it is my hope that its community of writers and readers can develop a way to keep things alive in cyberspace. In addition, the significant ability to embed various types of media within a hypertext document suggests that truly innovative treatments of the martial arts can incorporate the written word, sound, and video. One of the real challenges of "writing sword" is that what we are writing about is largely experiential in nature. Telling is useful, but seeing (and doing) even more so. Quality martial arts writing in the digital age should increasingly integrate multimedia digital technology to more effectively communicate, demonstrate, and explain. Such an approach will not only ensure a greater audience, since it aligns with trends in contemporary communication and consumer preferences, but will also reinforce my earlier plea for more team-based projects in which content experts join forces with those masters of the digital dojo.

Over the last twenty years, the *Journal of Asian Martial Arts*, through the guidance of its editor, Mike DeMarco, has been a (if not *the*) major vehicle to gather quality research and writing on the Asian martial arts, to disseminate it to an expanding community of practitioners and researchers, and to advocate for the point of view that this work is not only valuable in and of itself, but it also makes a significant contribution to the expanding ways in which we think about being human.

It has not always been easy. What we have written sometimes may not have been as effective as we would have wished. But in the pages of *JAMA* over the last two decades we have seen growing maturity and sophistication in the ways we think about the arts, as well as skill in the ways we write about them. In the pursuit of this Way, we experience the all-too-familiar events that mark progress along the martial path: constant challenge, and frequent frustration, yet deep gratification. It has been a privilege to walk this path with so many readers and fellow writers. In the end, we share a common experience and a common conviction. And at the end of a weary journey, we look up and glimpse something in the distance that continues to beckon.

One path may end. The journey never does.

*Illustration by Oscar Ratti.*

# Asian Martial Arts History From One Era to the Next

Robert E. Dohrenwend, Ph.D.

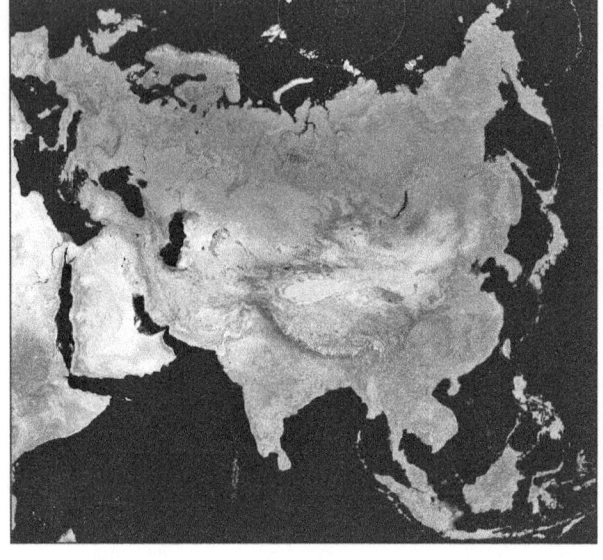

Since the end of the Second World War, there has been an explosive increase worldwide in the popularity of the Asian martial arts. Led by judo and Shotokan karate, instruction in these arts spread rapidly to North America, Europe, Australia, and New Zealand. These arts have fascinating histories, which attracted a great deal of interest. Thanks to a number of very able historians, we have come to know a great deal about developments in the martial arts during the twentieth and the latter part of the nineteenth centuries. The *Journal of Asian Martial Arts* played a significant role in making that history accessible to a wide readership.

Part of the fascination with martial arts history comes from factors that severely limit or distort much of the data concerning their earlier history. To begin with, there is often very little early authentic documentation for those periods, and that documentation may be hard to find. Any serious historian of the martial arts in Asia must be intimately familiar with the languages and cultures of the martial arts he studies. This allows him access to available primary documents, and permits contact with sources of valuable oral traditions. The case of Chinese is particularly frustrating. The language is difficult for those who have been brought up in western European cultures, and the colorful expressions often used to describe particular techniques or moves are anything but exact.

It is often said that there are no secrets in the martial arts. Rubbish! The history of the martial arts is the history of secrets grudgingly revealed. It could not be otherwise. The martial arts are coached skills, and although physical and physiological principles cannot be kept secret, specific techniques for their application can. All of the fighting arts have their origins in serious combat; experience and observations were formulated for systematic instruction to give students an advantage in their next fight. Not surprisingly, the techniques taught were regarded as secret. Surprising your enemy, confronting him with the unexpected, gives you a significant advantage in combat. In the past, such intentional secrecy has always been integral to martial arts instruction.

The unarmed fighting arts were traditionally taught to a small number of students, and individual instruction was the rule. It has often been the case that the complete teachings of various styles were only passed on from the head of the style to one student. If that student were to die before transmission of that knowledge was complete, the style might easily die out, leaving little trace of its existence. This could occur as a result of social disaster (China's Great Proletarian Cultural Revolution of the sixties is a good example), of natural catastrophe, or of war. A relatively modern example of this latter hazard occurred on Okinawa, when Miyagi Chojun's selected successor died toward the end of World War II.

The martial arts are the subject of many exaggerated legends, which attribute extraordinary and often supernatural skills to legendary masters. These stories are traditionally used for entertainment purposes in China, and Chinese acrobats are trained specifically in their stage presentation. This is also the case for European actors who must duel with swords on stage or screen, although the supernatural plays far less of a role. This use is harmless, but such impossible exploits may also be attributed to historical masters of the fighting arts. These exaggerations must be discounted without distorting the genuine accomplishments of some truly remarkable people. This is not easy.

As modern societies and values change everywhere with the increasing density of human population, we find that the martial arts have often changed their original purpose and practice, remarkably so in some cases, to more closely match modern social values. Deadly techniques are eliminated for safety in competition and to avoid litigation. Individual instruction has been abandoned for the large classes necessary for commercial success. Difficult techniques are eliminated to retain as many students as possible. These distortions in the modern martial arts make it more difficult to trace historical influences among the martial arts through related aspects of technical instruction.

Not only the arts themselves, but interpretations of their history have been altered to better agree with modern sensibilities, or to conform with recent nationalistic priorities. Historical accounts have been altered or suppressed to support these fictions, and there has been a great deal of deliberate falsification and pure invention to give some very recent martial arts or styles the luster of an ancient, if spurious, pedigree. All too often, instructors in those styles uncritically and enthusiastically accept this clumsy nonsense, and the excessive veneration they are accorded by many of their students makes it much harder to find out what really happened.

Although we know very little about ultimate origins, it is useful to separate the armed from the unarmed martial arts. The earliest human weapon known is the throwing spear, as we have good examples from Schöningen, Germany, reliably dated to ca. 400,000 years ago. The earliest documentation for any systematic unarmed martial art is that for the Greek Pankration around 700–600 BCE. We may tentatively conclude that the armed martial arts are far older than the unarmed, and that those weapons originated as hunting tools. It would be imprudent to go any further.

For example, we may suggest that systems for unarmed combat evolved from wrestling matches for entertainment and tribal status. This implies a very early origin involving struggles to establish rank and dominance for access to food and reproductive opportunity. However, unarmed combat styles may also have arisen from a perceived need for effective self-defense during periods when weapons were denied or otherwise unavailable to other than an armed elite. If this is the case, then the unarmed martial arts have a much later origin than weapon arts, but the need for secrecy in instruction is still obvious. Perhaps both explanations are correct. Perhaps neither is. These points require further investigation, as we really don't know.

Although we cannot state that systematic instruction in the unarmed martial arts originated in Greece, available evidence still suggests a line of transmission from Greece through the Middle East to India via the armies of Alexander the Great, around 325 BCE; adoption of a form of the Pankration in India; and later transmission of the Greek/Indian martial arts to China. There is no real evidence for the transmission of unarmed martial arts from India to China, but the Bodhidharma myth suggests that it may have occurred when Buddhism was introduced to China during the Tang dynasty (618–907).

Although the Shaolin myth is highly suspect, we may hypothesize that Indian fighting techniques then blended with indigenous Chinese ones to form a major Chinese style, which influenced all others. Chinese influence became probably important and even definitive for the origin and development of any early Korean unarmed martial arts, which seem to have faded during the nineteenth century. Early Chinese influences on Japan were also strong and persistent, but here they seem to have blended with well-established indigenous traditions. We know that Okinawan karate has important recent Chinese roots, and that Japanese karate is a very recent modification of the Okinawan art. The modern Korean martial arts are almost entirely Japanese in origin and very recent. This hypothetical line of development and transmission is plausible but still very shaky. Unfortunately, the available data and documentation do not permit anything more solid.

There are numerous martial traditions that developed independently from the main Asian traditions; for example, Capoeira in Brazil, English quarterstaff techniques and boxing, Sambo in Russia, and Savate and *la canne* in France. Subsequently, some of these "outside" traditions had significant influence on Asian martial traditions. For example, we have the European Renaissance sword fighting traditions and fencing, which so strongly influenced the Philippine style of arnis that another name for that art is *esgrima*, the Spanish word for "fencing." European cane fighting developed into a fighting arts ryu in late nineteenth-century Japan by Uchida Ryugoro (1837–1921) which became Uchida-ryu Tanjojutsu. The only Japanese weapons art of European origin, it is now taught as a supplement to the instruction given in Shindo Muso-ryu Jojutsu.

The influence was not all one way. In the later part of the nineteenth century, E.W. Barton-Wright, an Englishman, modified Japanese jujutsu to develop his own style of self-defense, Bartitsu, which enjoyed a considerable if brief vogue before the First World War. One of his instructors, Pierre Vigny, developed a style of stick fighting that has had more widespread and lasting influence.

Sadly, with the demise of the *Journal of Asian Martial Arts*, a window into the past has been closed. But "finding things out" is enormous fun and addictive behavior. Future historians will discover fascinating new stories to tell, and significant insights into human behavior from the study of martial arts history. The study of martial arts history is an intellectual feast, and we have only been able to sample a few of the dishes here. For example, just this brief overview suggests that a martial art may appear in any culture at any time, sometimes related to martial arts in other cultures and influenced by them. It suggests that the gradual development of a martial tradition and eventually a body of systematic techniques that we may call a martial art is a natural development to be expected in any culture with a strong identity. These are certainly interesting hypotheses. If verified, they will have identified a universal property characteristic of human cultures.

# Fists and Phantoms:
# Martial Arts and Media

James Grady, B.A.

Martial arts create experiences of touch. Media create information phantoms. Make enough media, and in it our primal urge to fight appears: cave paintings, Elizabethan ballads, woodblock prints by Japanese masters like Kuniyoshi. Fictions: novels, plays, movies, TV, *manga*. Journalism, histories, instructional DVDs, and websites—even rock and roll. The mix is especially pronounced in the subject *JAMA* has chronicled for twenty years: Asian martial arts.

Yet many Asian martial arts founders were barely media scarred or savvy—say illiterate Chinese "village artists" who perhaps drew on techniques from travelers to India, or from the village just over the horizon's fog-shrouded mountain. These village artists did not consult media to develop their art. They passed their art on by direct, usually painful, instruction. As late as the twentieth century, martial arts legends whose work lives on after them like Yang Chengfu were at best "media captured" by others' cameras and memoirs.

Media rose in power with scroll writings by scholar-monks from the Alps to the Himalayas, and became a cultural conveyer with the invention of paper by the first-century Han court eunuch Cai Lun. That made writing and painting easily portable. Johannes Guttenberg's printing press in 1439 put media on an exponential rate of increase in accessibility. By 1827, when Joseph Niepce made the first photograph, media daily influenced the "civilized" world. When radio, telephone, telegraph, and photography combined to create "motion pictures" and television, media went from a tool of humanity to a causal force for humanity—an empowerment magnified by the advent of personal computers and internet connectivity, helping turn us into cultural savant Marshall McLuhan's global village.

The title of McLuhan's seminal 1967 work, *The Medium Is the Message*, hints at why the embrace of media and martial arts was inevitable: touch, the defining experience of martial arts.

The power of media's phantoms is linked to their ability to "touch" consumers—intellectually as a seductive argument and emotionally in a portrayal we can identify with. The more universally visceral our identification, the more powerful the media's impact.

Everybody's been hit. Everybody's thought about hitting somebody. The

*Illustration courtesy of 123RF Stock Photo • Photography by Kheng Ho Toh.*

hitting touch is the heart of martial arts. Media makers know that—and want to empower their media.

Scholars/martial artists John Corcoran and Emil Farkas document the fusion of Asian martial arts and media back to 720 A.D. and the *Nihon Shoki*, a chronicle of Japanese history. Beyond paintings and fictions, with exceptions like judo founder Kano Jigaro's early twentieth-century works, martial arts emerged in media mostly via quasi-journalistic fashions right up through the 1950s, when boys across America stumbled on "how to" books on judo in public libraries. Karate leapt into the mass media about that same time—notably in Ian Fleming's 1959 James Bond novel *Goldfinger*—with black and white photo-filled how-to books entering mass circulation by the mid-1960s. Memoir/instruction books by venerable martial artists like Taiji's Zheng Manqing (with Robert Smith) and karate's Funakoshi Gichin didn't commonly appear in bookstores until the late 1960s, as ever more martial artists learned to use media to preserve something of what they'd learned for future generations.

But "motionless media" like print, painting, and photography do not account for the enormous impact of the martial arts–media embrace. The media symbolized by Hollywood—movies, TV, and now cyber systems like "webisodes" —captured the kinetic drama of martial arts and created that enormous impact. Importantly—ironically—the media that slammed martial arts into our global consciousness is media that does not portray reality: filmed fictions.

Hollywood has loved martial arts since 1921's cinematic drama *Outside Woman*, which featured a jujutsu-skilled Japanese manservant. Martial arts give filmed entertainment conflict, action, and a visual way to imbue characters with heroic or evil attributes. Listing good or bad Hollywood productions of martial arts is fun folly: new movies come out every week, so lists quickly grow incomplete. But such lists show an exponential rate of increase in movies where martial arts appear, which means media expose ever more billions of people to "information dumps" about martial arts.

And so in the twentieth century, our global culture embraced the idea that there's something called "martial arts." Media exposure equaled cultural ratification.

With martial arts expert and media creator John Donohue, I assert that so far, the most important "martial arts movie" is the *Star Wars* saga, where concepts of warrior training fused with "the Force" mimic Asian martial arts with their concepts of *qi/ki*.

Martial arts' media magnification/ratification coincided with America's cultural infatuation with other "Asian" concepts like Buddhism, bushido, Daoism, the *Kama Sutra*, yoga, and Zen, an infatuation intertwined with the sixties countercultural rejection of the white, male-dominated "man in the gray flannel suit" cliché. In post-9/11 America that cliché became successfully reimagined for the same aging sixties countercultural set and their successors by the TV series *Mad Men*.

But flashing back to the sixties, to paraphrase media maker and gongfu adept Charles Johnson, you didn't need to be Buddhist to practice Asian martial arts (though martial arts led him to Buddhism). JAMA editor Russ Mason has pointed out that martial arts need not conflict with other religions, such as Christianity. Bruce Lee, whose existence represents the *über absurdum* of the martial arts–media embrace, noted: "Before I studied, a punch to me was just a punch. After I'd studied, a punch was no longer a punch. Now that I understand the art, a punch is just a punch." Still, the journey from the tangible practicality of martial arts to a philosophical epiphany is common.

But that journey is often misunderstood. Many people see martial arts explode on their movie screens, and not only (as Donohue and I assert) is it often their first exposure to such physical realities, but those physical realities—or rather their media phantoms—often lead people to think that an acquaintanceship with martial arts will automatically and quickly convey enlightenment, give them calm and peace, success and fulfillment—plus the ability to kick ass. With the right uniform and a few classes, perhaps they can magically transform who they are and become the heroic media "phantom."

The tipping point for the martial arts–media embrace came when the movie *Billy Jack* (1971) and the TV series *Kung Fu* (1972–75) featured martial arts as a central force instead of a "bit" in their fictions, creating a wave of cultural consciousness—and craving.

For example, in September 1973, the sensei and roughly twenty veteran members of the University of Montana karate club were stunned at the academic year's first practice for their group: more than two hundred male and female newbies showed up. By week 3 of ordinary training that included push-ups, 90 percent of those seekers had moved on from this realm of sweat and pain.

Media made martial arts popular and therefore more accessible, while martial arts made consumers with cash for media. Getting that cash means media's content of martial arts is often commercialized junk or glitter: the goal for media is content consumption, not comprehensive representation.

Martial arts are about touch that involves work, sweat, and an investment in loss. Practicing martial arts requires you to be here, now. Or get hit. Media conveys phantom martial arts encounters with no such difficulty. Consuming media requires you only to open the necessary intake senses.

That disconnection creates perilous confusion from barroom bluffs to playground mishaps. While media learning can augment physical study, seeing a hundred martial arts movies does not automatically teach you how to handle one back-alley encounter.

Now as we hurtle into the future—and as *JAMA* bows out—media is expanding into science-fiction scenarios. Google's Project Glass portrays a day in the life of a person wearing glasses that present media from photos to maps to TV-quality live chats. Google's preview has, as of this writing, more than thirteen million views on YouTube. Even *The New York Times* knows this means something important. Perhaps martial arts and its embrace with media point to what.

Media beyond twenty-first-century gaming systems like Wii will make it possible to "be" in a martial arts encounter regardless of your physicality or physical presence. When future media creators "jack in," they might provide us with "experiences" that trigger our jacked-in neural system so we can "feel" ourselves knocking out Bruce Lee.

But we won't be in a real "there." We'll be phantoms, with perhaps some few of us also searching out old-fashioned, marginally popular, sweat-smelling *guans* and dojos where we can learn from real human touch.

Let's hope some *JAMA*-level media is there to chronicle that for the next future.

# An Optimal Elixir: Blending Spiritual, Healing, and Combative Components

Michael Maliszewski, Ph.D.

The *Journal of Asian Martial Arts* (JAMA) was being introduced at the time I was completing a ten-year research project dealing with meditative practices and indigenous healing traditions. The project had originally started out as a short article addressing the one-sided focus on physical combat that appeared to dominate much of the martial arts at that time. As a core focus of my work, I had traveled throughout many Asian countries to track down information on the medical and more esoteric side. In addition, I attended a plethora of martial arts seminars on all the major and some minor systems I had read about to get an insider's intellectual view and in-body felt sense of the particular tradition. It also allowed me to meet all kinds of practitioners—from martial arts masters to film actors and producers. There were so many traditions and so many mythologies and legends that it was hard to tease out which were authentic or historically valid. Most writings ended up being published in popular magazines, and there was no central source where a rigorous academic treatise could be published—that is, until Mike DeMarco offered a legitimate forum for a scholar-practitioner of the arts.

Reflecting on the evolution of martial arts now, some twenty years since my work was published in the journal, there have been a number of trends. Mixed martial arts have become quite popular, eclipsing the interest level of other Western sports traditionally associated with the U.S. I believe, however, there has been a decline in the depth that has characterized the more traditional systems. The spiritual or meditative focus is more "generic" in the sense that any loose association with the ethereal is deemed spiritual or metaphysical. Even in nonmartial "spiritual" traditions such as yoga, the focus is now on postures and exercises for physical development rather than the rigorous psychophysical exercises designed to achieve a higher state of consciousness—the core focus of traditional yoga.

In general martial arts study today, practitioners do not have the dedication to endure the long hours of training required to reach a level of authentic mastery in a tradition. There are many teachers setting up schools with limited real training or skill. Even on a superficial level dealing with media and entertainment,

Photograph courtesy of Marvin Labbate.

there are few enduring icons in martial arts. Many have passed on. New champions appear in mixed martial arts every few months. I began my research because many of the teachers I met at the time felt their knowledge of the esoteric and spiritual would be lost, as even their best students had no interest in these realms. Their impressions turned out to be rather true. There has developed a burgeoning interest in alternative health and integrative medicine but, ironically, this appears largely outside of martial arts proper, where the close connection between combat and healing had been held for centuries. It is sad to see the journal come to an end, but perhaps JAMA's archive of published articles will spur on a future reader and martial artist on the path of self-discovery.

**Which Way to the Source?**

Given the limitations I have pointed out above, a question that arises is how to gain access to information related to spiritual practices. There are several directions one can take, akin to what might parallel "reverse engineering."

One direction is to explore the vast array of meditative traditions. Aside from computer searches, college courses in the history of religions or psychology of religion at local colleges can offer good source material. One can get direct teachings in different systems from seminars in specific traditions or local centers that offer such training. Supplemental meditative practices can be integrated into one's martial arts. Finding authentic teachers may require detailed searches, but the tenacious investigator can accomplish it.

On the healing arts, traditional healing approaches can also be explored on the internet. As noted earlier, many hospitals and medical centers are now exploring integrative medicine and alternate health practices. The most visible healthcare modalities at this time are acupuncture, reiki, yoga, and different forms of body therapy, including massage. Developing expertise in these practices can be readily integrated into martial arts practice.

For the more dedicated and perseverant, travel to Asian countries to meet with elder teachers of different traditions can be most fruitful. This is not an easy task, and it involves substantial preparation to track down authentic masters. Initial investigations may begin as an academic exercise, or by attending seminars. Eventually, personal encounters with different practitioners will provide a direction to follow. Also, try to track down authors who have published books or papers in areas of interest that appeared in JAMA. Most writers maintain an interest in what they wrote and are happy to pass along resources to pursue further work. Personal introductions by those with contacts already established can prove extremely valuable.

## Caution: Fool's Gold Ahead

While I have outlined above a general roadmap one might follow, I would also caution the reader that there is no clear-cut picture as to how one's path of exploration might unfold. Common stereotypes may not hold weight as the journey to discovery of internal, external, and spiritual aspects of the martial arts unfolds. I say this from experience. My earliest inquiries were "precomputer" and necessitated travel throughout the U.S., Europe, and Asia to track down information that could not generally be found in popular articles or academic books. Assumptions I had concluded from my own readings were often dispelled. For example, although various martial traditions in Asia were historically associated with religious traditions (e.g., Buddhism, Daoism), practitioners often had limited knowledge of these traditions and their extensive spiritual practices.

I discovered that physical mastery does not necessarily have a direct relation to spiritual practices, just as a high level of spiritual attainment does not guarantee physical mastery. I concluded that no singular image or profile of physical, personal, or spiritual development constituted a highly evolved master of both martial and meditative traditions. Practitioners had certain strengths and weaknesses concerning spiritual practices and goals; their skills varied regarding physical exercises, techniques, and forms. There is also no acknowledged consensus on who is or what constitutes the highest level of mastery in martial, spiritual or meditative practices themselves.

## Spiritual Aspects and What We Perceive

To digress, I share some experiences with people I have known. Robert Smith told me his coauthor, Donn Draeger, avoided meeting with some of his Chinese masters when the opportunity presented itself. Draeger focused more on the external aspects of the arts.

Smith himself was not impressed with Bruce Lee and his Jeet Kune Do. According to Lee's earlier students, Lee used meditative techniques to enhance his physical performance in the martial arts. By contrast, Vladimir Vasiliev, founder of Systema, had a background training in the KGB and roots in Russian orthodox Christianity the latter of which had no connection with his unorthodox system of training and exercises. Jesse Glover, an early student of Lee in Seattle, saw Vasiliev in action and said he probably could have defeated Lee. Other later Lee students have concluded Systema to be of limited value.

Ueshiba Morihei had a highly developed spiritual experience, and this affected his physical skill. I met a former Olympic medal winner in judo from Japan who encountered Ueshiba when he was in his prime and was given the challenge to move the diminutive Ueshiba as he sat on the floor in *seiza* (kneeling position). The Olympian, who weighed nearly two hundred pounds, was unable to do so.

Many other examples could be described here, but this is the general picture of what one may find. So, in conclusion, there exist a myriad of different possibilities as to how to look at these practices and systems as one sets out to self-discovery in the martial arts.

Photographs © iStockphoto.com

## Drinking the Elixir

There exist many different types of meditation. Most static meditation can be divided into concentration, mindfulness, or a combination of both. Some of the internal martial arts systems, such as Taijiquan, have been described as "moving meditation," in contrast to the nonmartial forms (although both concentration and mindfulness techniques can be performed in motion). A sample exercise for concentration meditation would involve focusing attention exclusively on one object and preventing the mind from wandering elsewhere. A mindfulness technique would involve sitting quietly and observing—while breathing normally—the passage of air in and out of the tip of the nose, simply witnessing the sensation and process and not responding to it. Mindfulness practices have become very popular in psychotherapy.

Distinctions between martial meditative practice and strict nonmartial sitting meditation practices were reviewed in my earlier paper (Maliszewski, 1992: 35–44) and may be of interest to the reader. To develop internal, energy-based capabilities, students might seek out energy-based healing or meditative systems and have the internal energy transmitted to them if an authentic qigong system is not readily available. One such system is reiki, which has become popular in many hospital settings with nursing departments. The internal healing energy could be combined with any martial arts system. The direction that can follow depends upon the focus and goals of the practitioner. The physical practice of martial arts (especially internal-designated systems) can accelerate the speed with which one can experience advanced states of consciousness in meditation. Despite changes in the world today, resources for pursuing an authentic spiritual path still do exist for those seeking to make this journey.

The practitioner seeking a greater sense of spirituality and meaning in the world can find that martial arts offer much in terms of development of one's personal character. A simple adage to follow is that the focus of what you put into the practice will yield the fruits of your labor. The discipline required to practice repeated exercises or forms and adhere to a code of moral behavior will strengthen both body and mind, providing the necessary grounding and foundation needed to develop and affirm one's sense of self. The heightened awareness that emerges over time through more advanced practice will lead to a greater ability to focus attention, not only on specific movements, but also toward awareness of one's mental processes and emotional state. The introduction of sitting meditation as a complement to moving meditation will facilitate the development of noncorporeal experiences where one's consciousness is expanded to include atypical states of consciousness that comprise the spiritual domain of our existence in the world.

MALISZEWSKI, M. (1992). Meditative-religious traditions of fighting arts and martial ways. *Journal of Asian Martial Arts*, 1(3): 1–104. Part III, Martial disciplines and meditative traditions, pages 35–44.

*Illustration courtesy of iStockphoto.com • Photography by Viktor Levi.*

# Academic Research into Chinese Martial Arts: Problems and Perspectives

Kai Filipiak, Ph.D.

The following article aims to discuss the present state of academic research into Chinese martial arts. I was asked to provide "constructive thoughts" that could help to name the weaknesses existing in this field. Instead of simply complaining about many shortcomings, I would like to name some problems, discuss their causes, and present perspectives to deal with them.

Let me start with the institutionalization of academic research in general. Members of the academic community are currently faced with an increasing global trend to economize. This has not only a deep impact on universities and other academic institutions, but also on scientific work. In times of the increasing role of third-party funds to finance academic research, one has to take into account the consequences when choosing a topic outside the mainstream.

That may be one reason the field of martial arts is largely ignored by the academic world. As a result, the decision for martial arts as a research project poses a significant risk for young scholars, who will find little support and little acceptance. Another reason scholars pay little attention to the topic is related to the practical side of martial arts. Sometimes it is useful to have a rough idea of the technical aspects, even when dealing with the historical, social, and cultural problems of the phenomenon.

There is no solution for the "institutional" problems in the foreseeable future, but I would advocate for more networking among researchers. We should also be open to those who study martial arts in other areas of Asia to emphasize the importance of the topic. Finally, we should look for new forms of cooperation. For example, the growing field of Chinese military history could be an important platform to present results to a broader audience.

Let us now turn to some problems concerning the contents of research. Scholars concerned with the history of Chinese martial arts should be aware of different imbalances in the field. It is quite obvious that there are temporal, spatial, and style-related imbalances. The majority of projects have focused on late imperial China, which means the time of the Ming (1368–1644) and Qing (1644–1911) dynasties. This is not surprising because the majority of existing sources date back to these periods. In addition, the Ming-Qing period was a formative time for many styles that influence our perception of Chinese martial arts today. In contrast, too little is known about Chinese martial arts in pre-Ming times.

Moreover, with respect to perception, we need a more precise definition what *martial arts* really are. The term was originally applied to forms of fighting in East Asia, and it describes a modern phenomenon of cultural significance. Later the impression was given that this art of fighting has a long history with origins we can trace back to the Neolithic period. But there is a large gap between throwing stones and attacking the head with your leg. Actually, we have no idea when Chinese martial arts began, and this problem is also related to terminology. Most people talking about Chinese martial arts have in mind popular styles such as Shaolin, Taiji, Bagua, and others. They do not keep in mind that these complex systems are the products of the very late period of Chinese history.

Another question concerns the contents of Chinese martial arts. What defines the Chinese way of fighting to be an *art*, and what includes and excludes martial arts? For example, there were large differences between the military form of fighting and forms practiced by martial artists in terms of function, use, teaching, concepts, and weapons. Of course, there were also relations and exchanges between both. In addition, one could ask why modern competitions of forms (*taolu* 套路) are named as *martial arts*. In fact, the movements are acrobatic and fascinating, but hardly of use for fighting.

The focus on extant popular styles caused another imbalance in the field. As a result, the role of the Shaolin monastery or the village Chenjiagou for the development of Chinese martial arts is overestimated. For example, there is evidence for martial practice in many Buddhist locations. There were many cases of collective martial violence in medieval Chinese Buddhism. This opens a wide field for academic research, which should systematically explore the relationship between violence and Buddhism, martial traditions of Chinese monasteries and the military use of fighting monks.

The second religion that has been related to Chinese martial arts is Daoism, but historical evidence for Daoist practice of martial arts is rare. Attempts in modern research to apply concepts of martial arts to Daoist origins are almost anachronistic. For example, in Chinese history the concept of qi was a general concept used in different philosophical, medical, and religious contexts. Qigong exercises were as well part of different traditions. We do not know when exactly qigong became part of martial arts practice, nor from which tradition it was taken. The example shows clearly that we must carefully examine the origins of traditional concepts and their relevance for martial arts.

CHINESE SOLDIERS AT THE TIME OF THE BOXER REBELLION. PD-US

The focus on the various locations with different martial arts traditions should also include a closer look to China's minorities. During its long history, China became a multiethnic empire that suppressed, integrated, and assimilated other cultures. Non-Chinese from the North and South served the emperor as elite soldiers. They had their own martial traditions and contributed to Chinese martial arts. Therefore, the investigation of Chinese martial arts should include a multiethnic perspective.

In addition, we need a more systematic approach to the written sources, one based on textual analyses and criticism, the history of editions, the verifying of related styles and individuals, and the evaluation of texts for the history of martial arts. In short, we need far more carefully annotated translations.

There is also a lack of sociohistorical milieu studies that make use of the wide variety of sources that could help us to understand different forms of organization related to martial arts, such as the family, village militias, community compacts, army, organizations of different professions (artists, traders, smugglers, bodyguards, beggars), monasteries, robber bands, private gentry troops, and their relations with each other. We need to know more about motivations and objectives of practitioners, their carriers, and their roles inside these organizations.

We know a little bit about martial arts practiced by members of the Boxer Rebellion in 1900, but we know almost nothing on the role of martial arts during the Taiping Rebellion (1851–1864), one of the largest uprisings in the world ever. However, martial arts were not only part of Chinese popular culture. There were members of the elite who had a passion for martial objects. They collected armors and weapons, and some of them practiced martial arts. Investigations into the role of martial arts within the elite and relations between literates and martial artists could help to adjust our perception of the pacifistic, literature-oriented elite who paid little heed to military skills and detested all forms of physical training.

Although the dimension of historical research to Chinese martial arts is still limited, there are an increasing number of studies that reflect the significance of martial arts for traditional Chinese culture. For example, martial narratives became part of literary studies that investigate different genres, the role of martial heroes, and related gender constructions. These studies provide a welcome opportunity to learn more about the popularity of martial arts in Chinese society and their function in different cultural contexts. Much more could be done to explore the role of martial arts in opera, drama, shadow theater, music, fine arts, and other fields.

Compared to other Chinese forms of physical culture, martial arts have survived until the present day. Together with other Asian martial arts, Chinese martial arts became popular around the world and contributed greatly to overcome Western perceptions of China as backward. The role of martial arts during the process of globalization provides a large field for academic research. The process began with the reshaping of martial arts under the influence of Western sports during the nineteenth century. It caused the classification of martial arts into "traditional" and "modern" martial arts. The latter included the transformation of martial arts into sport, but it did not find international recognition. With respect to the adaptation of martial arts to modernity, we have to be more aware of the pros and cons of the process. It would also be interesting to figure out why other sports, for example Taekwondo, were more successful.

On the other hand, Chinese martial arts produced global brands, such as "Shaolin Kungfu," that were able to influence Western cultures. So-called Shaolin temples were established around the world, promoting the commercialization and mythologization of martial arts. Skills and techniques of Chinese martial arts became a basic part of Western movies. Analysis of martial arts should open new perspectives on the globalization process and its actors in the East and West, as well as forms of exchanges and mutual influences. This analysis should help to establish a broader perception of Chinese martial arts as an integral part of global martial arts.

# Nicks and Cuts:
# Continuing Endeavors in Japanese Budo

Dave Lowry, B.A.

The confusion was reasonable. JAMA? Where was the research on Peruvian Meteorite Syndrome? The summation of the study on retroviruses? Ah, no. This JAMA was devoted to the combat disciplines of Asia.

I contributed two articles and my share of book reviews over the years. The editor even indulged me in reviewing a classic treatise on Noh. I did not write more articles, one reason being that the curricula vitae of regular contributors—Ph.Ds and their ilk—would have made my relatively modest college accomplishments look, well, modest. And I read it. We all did. There were few serious martial arts enthusiasts who did not regularly peruse JAMA, if not through subscription then by indulging in that time-honored means of reading, what the Japanese call *tachi-yomi*—standing and turning pages at the bookstore.

When JAMA began, there was little formal scholarship on the Asian fighting arts. Other magazines, devoted to more popular aspects of these arts, occasionally published something of note. Not often. What JAMA sought was to elevate the subject. To give it the heft and seriousness of any other worthy scholarship.

In a sense, JAMA sought, in periodical form, to take the path blazed by the late Donn Draeger and his colleagues back in the early seventies. Draeger perceived in the combat arts of Asia a fascinating, multilayered field of scholarly inquiry that had never been taken seriously by any researchers of Asian culture. Draeger endeavored to address that lacuna. His efforts were directed at cataloguing the panoply of these arts, categorizing them efficiently, explaining them authoritatively, exploring their nuances, their strategies. He largely created the field of study; he named it as well: hoplology.

Probably the earliest publication that could be considered a predecessor to JAMA was *Judo Illustrated*, a handsome, professionally produced periodical, staffed by Draeger and his cohort: Phil Relnick, Quintin Chambers, Pascal Krieger, Meik Skoss, Liam Keeley, Hunter Armstrong, and others. It was full of engrossing articles, interviews, with technical pieces as well. It lasted about five issues.

Oh, it lasted longer than that. But not much. Publication costs were daunting. Most of the contributors were living in Asia; getting the magazine into the hands of readers in the West was challenging, unreliable. And Draeger's untimely death in 1982, which also changed ambitious plans for a hoplology research center at the University of Hawaii, signaled an end as well to any real efforts at publishing.

© *Illustration by Oscar Ratti.*

For many years, the scholarly books and periodicals devoted to combat arts written in English would have fit comfortably on a single bookshelf. A few titles appeared from time to time. Karl Friday and William Bodiford, both professors, published well-researched books on the history and culture of Japan's warrior class. *Hoplos*, a fitfully published journal, continued in Draeger's spirit for some years after he inaugurated it. Diane Skoss's publishing company, Koryu Books, produced three volumes on the classical martial arts of Japan that will remain definitive for many years. Wayne Muromoto's wonderful quarterly, *Furyu*, was a must read during its published life.

In 1991 Michael DeMarco came up with a notion that was both new —serious martial arts literature?—and a continuation of the hoplological devotions of Draeger and others.

Did it work? Well, yes. In some sense. It worked well. It was thick, professionally produced. One needed only to heft an issue, to gauge its weight, to know this was not going to be something directed at the enthusiasms of a fifteen-year-old boy.

Serious martial artists were initially skeptical. Some articles were outside the norm, dealing with unfamiliar topics and styles. There were some remarkable submissions. Among the best retrospectives on the Taiwanese Hong Yixiang. Allen Pittman's superb article on Bagua's single-palm change. Joseph Svinth's engaging history of kendo in Canada. Ellis Amdur's explanation of Maniwa Nen-ryu. JAMA has far more to be proud of than to be embarrassed about, no small feat when dealing with arts that are so liable to misinterpretation or misrepresentation. If you do not, like many of us, have these issues close at hand, they are available for online purchase. And you should.

And so, where does it go from here? To say that the conclusion of JAMA's publication leaves a hole in the field of the Asian combat arts scholarship is an understatement, obviously. It is interesting that in its final iteration, the magazine transformed itself almost entirely to a digital format. It's significant. There is more information available online about the fighting arts of China, Japan, and the rest of East Asia than one could read in six lifetimes. And we're not talking about the nonsense—of which there is also a staggering accumulation. No, we mean reliable, authoritative works, articles, blogs, opinion pieces, entire books, all online, all available for the energy expended of clicking a few keys.

It is impossible for the younger reader to comprehend how extraordinary this is. It is equally impossible for my generation to explain how foreign this is. Some perspective: In 1969 the first communication I got from Donn Draeger came in the form of a powder-blue airmail letter, one that had to be slit along its creased edges to open. It came nearly three months after I'd written him. What correspondence we shared until the end of his life was just as protracted in delivery. Today, when I have a question of one of my teachers or my seniors thousands of miles away, I tap it out, click and—it's there.

For better and worse—it is both—the scholarly future of combat-arts research will be as much revealed on a screen as in books; manuscripts; and ancient, rolled scrolls. This is particularly true of the Japanese martial arts.

There are young men and women living as longtime Japan residents now. Their scholarship, frankly, has in many ways exceeded that of Draeger and others of earlier generations. There are reasons for this: they have had superior access to learning the language, to apprenticing to budo masters there. As I write, an American has just been asked to assume the role of headmaster of a very traditional martial ryu. And he will be groomed for the position by other Americans, who are also senior in the ryu. These martial artists have achieved more, in breadth and depth—because of the efforts of those early researchers like Draeger.

It is all encouraging. The dissemination of information has never been easier. There have never been so many English-speaking authorities who can be consulted. Weathered, stained scrolls that were unrolled for scholars of the last generation in the chilly, musty storage rooms of old practitioners in some backwater region of Japan can now be studied on one's computer screen.

It is worthwhile to observe though—take it, please, from someone who has had those crusty old scrolls unrolled before him—that while the future of Japanese martial arts research may be conducted in the ether of the internet and in other computerized forms—the essence of these arts, their articulation, their true understanding, will come about just as they always have. Through perspiration, reflection, through an intimate relationship with a qualified teacher, through patience and a willingness to subsume one's ego.

The future of research in the Japanese martial arts and in the further understanding of them is apt to mutate in ways we cannot predict. Many of those in charge of the more obscure arts have concluded secrecy may not be in the best interest for the continued health of these arts. They open. The bulk of information that may soon be dumped for public consumption could be considerable. It will require a nimbleness of approach to put these in perspective. Future scholarship will also depend upon the study of these arts being given the attention of other scholars interested in Japan. The dismissal of the Japanese martial arts by academics has outlived any currency it may have had. JAMA has done much to lay the groundwork for more respect afforded to the martial arts in these circles.

JAMA has served a useful function in the maturation of the martial and fighting arts of Japan as they are practiced and understood and appreciated in the West. Its publication and history were a laudable undertaking. We'll miss it.

Though on a personal note, I never did find in its pages that article on *palastaie limosae* infections.

# The Ongoing Construction
# Linking Taekwondo with Academic Research

Willy Pieter, Ph.D.

The *Journal of Asian Martial Arts* (JAMA) has played an important role in disseminating scientific knowledge to coaches and practitioners about Taekwondo's perceived history and some of the scientific research that was carried out to assist them in their efforts to improve practice, performance, and health. The strength of JAMA has always been its efforts to make scientific research accessible to the lay person. It was a unique perspective when the journal first came out twenty years ago and remained so until this day.

Earlier than academic journals, JAMA debunked the "history" of Taekwondo. Although national and international Taekwondo governing bodies would like us to believe that the sport originated in antiquity, it actually started in the twentieth century, after World War II. Historical research showed that Taekwondo was influenced by karate and that it was not related to Taekkyon at all. The foot techniques in Taekkyon were borrowed from Taekwondo instead of the other way around. In a recent article in JAMA, it was shown that early Taekwondo techniques were based on Shotokan karate, which should not come as a surprise, since the pioneers of Taekwondo all learned karate in Japan. Interestingly, faculty at universities in Korea are well aware of Taekwondo's origin. All the more surprising is that both the Korean Taekwondo Association (KTA) and the World Taekwondo Federation (WTF) insist on propagating Taekwondo's

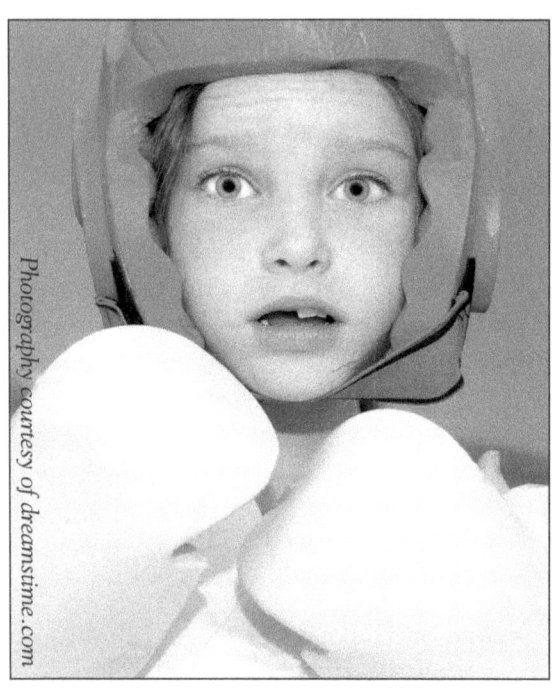

Photography courtesy of dreamstime.com

erroneous and misleading historical links.

JAMA also played an important role in providing the Taekwondo coach with tools to improve technique training through biomechanical information. Biomechanics is crucial for the coach to be able to teach skills properly, especially in combination with knowledge of motor learning. Pedagogical principles are important when dealing with children and youth, while they also provide guidelines for the most appropriate teaching methods. Children are not miniature adults and need a teaching approach suitable to their physical and mental development. This implies knowledge of growth and development as well as developmental psychology, motor control, and motor learning.

Research on assessing Taekwondo skills is lacking. What is the basis for deciding that a Taekwondo practitioner deserves to get the next belt? Traditional values to award belts need to be reassessed. For instance, what's the difference between a green and blue belt, or between a third and a seventh dan? So, if a first dan is supposed to execute the side kick in a certain way, how different is the side kick of a second or third dan? How about children? Children of the same age may differ developmentally, so how do we assess them? How is the same technique different between children and adults? If variations of the same technique are exhibited, do we have criteria to assess them? Would it not be better to get rid of the belt system in Taekwondo? It is a sport, and there are no belts in volleyball or gymnastics. Do biomechanical criteria ever enter the assessment of techniques during promotions for higher belt ranks, and, if so, do we have a template to apply this to those who gain more experience in Taekwondo?

JAMA also covered the psychological makeup of the Taekwondo athlete. Psychological factors have long been shown to play an important role in training and competition in many, if not all, sports. Near the end of a strenuous workout, the psychological makeup of the athletes will often determine if they will be able to go the distance. In competition, psychological factors frequently contribute to winning or losing. How do coaches prepare their athletes for competition? Is this different when dealing with children as opposed to adults?

How are psychological factors related to injuries in Taekwondo? Research on young-adult Taekwondo athletes revealed that losing injured females scored higher on anger, fatigue, and confusion. Fatigue in their male counterparts was also related to injury. On the other hand, anger was associated with winning performances in young-adult female karate athletes. It was suggested that they used anger to psych themselves up. Higher depression and fatigue were reported for losing male varsity Taekwondo athletes. However, the effect of anger on performance is suggested to be mediated by depression. In other words, only in nondepressed individuals will anger be positively related to performance. If tension and anger are high in a depressed group, they may lead to injury.

Injuries have been investigated from an epidemiological perspective. Cerebral concussions in Taekwondo have been found to be four times higher than in American football over a fifteen-year period. Some of these injuries have been fatal in American football, and media reports have also revealed deaths in Taekwondo. The youngest of these was seventeen years old. He had been practicing Taekwondo for a year and was kicked in the neck during competition by a fifteen-year-old who had more experience. In 1998, JAMA published an article in which serious injuries in karate and full-contact Taekwondo were compared. Serious injuries included bone fractures and cerebral concussions. Although the scientific community has stepped up its research on these types of injuries in contact sports in general, the WTF has failed to follow suit. In fact, over the years, the WTF has increased the points for kicks to the head/face from 1 to 4 points for a turning kick as of this writing. It is assumed that "turning" refers to a rotational kick. A kick that is not rotational but still hits the head scores 3 points. In the 1998 JAMA article, it was reported that a kick to the neck may rupture the carotid artery in the side of the neck, thereby restricting blood flow to the brain. Diminished blood flow to the brain results in brain damage or even death.

To gain better insight into the mechanics of concussions in Taekwondo, our team has initiated preliminary laboratory studies using a so-called anthropometric test dummy that is also used in studies on car crashes. These tests entail kicking a head and neck dummy that is instrumented with one or more accelerometers. Our initial results showed that the roundhouse kick yielded linear accelerations of 61–217g, while the axe kick recorded accelerations between 26–99g. One g equals 9.81 m/s2.* Both kicks have been most frequently implicated in concussions, with the roundhouse kick being the most often used technique in competition. The roundhouse kick also produced a faster acceleration than the hook punch in boxing.

Fractures and concussions in Taekwondo are of even greater concern when dealing with children and youth. American and Greek young Taekwondo athletes recorded 34% of all injuries to the head and neck, which is second to the lower extremities. Korean middle- and high-school children received more than one severe head blow in 28% of cases. A counterattack was at the basis of 44.3% of head blows, including those that resulted in a concussion.

* Acceleration is measured in "g," where 1 g corresponds to the vertical acceleration force due to gravity.

A recent article in JAMA reviewed performance-related characteristics of young Taekwondo athletes. Concern was expressed about grouping these young competitors according to their age rather than maturity. Since children of the same calendar age could include both early and late maturers, the wisdom of putting them in the same weight division must be questioned. In males, early maturers are stronger than their normal-maturing counterparts, let alone when compared to those who are late maturers. Research on American junior Taekwondo athletes revealed that the early maturers were taller, and their legs were also longer.

Despite rigged competition results at the international level, including the Olympic Games, as was recently admitted by a high-ranking official in the international Taekwondo governing body, it is still advisable to plan one's training properly to increase the chances of performing optimally. Planning training programs is a matter of theoretical knowledge, practical experience, and the athlete's potential. One can never be sure that the best plans will also result in the best outcome, but the chances of failure may be reduced. Some coaches do not seem to adhere to principles of periodization. It is not uncommon for their Taekwondo athletes to train seven days per week, 365 days per year. This approach has been shown to result in staleness, frequently resulting in reduced performance with an increased risk of sustaining injuries. Some of these injuries may end the athlete's competition career. In children, there is also the risk of fractures to the growth areas of the bones, which may lead to stunted growth.

JAMA embodied the link joining history, philosophy, science, and martial arts practitioners. The initiative twenty years ago was a novelty and showed insight that until then was largely unknown among many. The end of JAMA seems to indicate that some of us are not ready yet to take the next step to a deeper understanding of our martial arts of interest. To be an innovator is one of the challenges confronting humankind. Many are talented; only a few are unique. JAMA belongs to the latter category. When JAMA takes its final bow, the scientific community will have lost the bridge to the martial arts field and vice versa.

In Korea and other countries around the world, the study of martial arts has entered the academic curriculum. For instance, several Korean universities offer degree programs in Taekwondo. The students are admitted based on both their academic and Taekwondo acumen. Some of them are hoping to become coaches after their competition careers are over. Contrary to previous generations of coaches, the next one will also be academically educated. Viewed from that perspective, JAMA was way ahead of its time. Hopefully, the next generation will rebuild the bridge that JAMA started.

# The Whole Shebang
# Concerning Southeast Asian Martial Arts

Kirstin Pauka, Ph.D.

Martial arts in Southeast Asia have not received nearly as much attention in scholarly research as those of East Asia. Reasons for this might be historically found in the lesser degree of accessibility to Western practitioners, and in the consequently much sparser distribution of Southeast Asian training schools in the U.S. and Europe overall. Schools for Malay silat, Thai boxing, or Philippine arnis are still relatively rare compared with the abundance of Taijiquan, Taekwondo, or karate schools outside of their home countries. JAMA has been one of the first publications to provide a forum for research on some of these martial arts traditions. Yet much more remains to be done.

In the case of Malay and Indonesian martial arts, there are literally thousands of recognized regional styles of Pencak Silat, kuntao* and hybrid forms today; only a very small fraction thereof have ever been documented. A vast treasure trove of techniques, weaponry, and underlying philosophies remains to be discovered and cherished.

One of the unique features of silat in Indonesia that—in my opinion—warrants further study is the fact that it is practiced in connection with the five major religions found in the region. The strongest connection is of course with still vibrant and diverse practices of animism. In this context there is a strong bond linking silat, spiritual practices, ancestor worship, and healing arts. Emphasis here is placed on the development and refinement of internal power or knowledge, referred to generally as *ilmu batin* or *tenaga dalam*.

The second strongest connection is with Islam, especially with older and more mystical beliefs originating from the earliest introduced schools of Sufi Islam. Today silat is often taught in close proximity to or directly at *pesantren* (Islamic boarding schools).

Connections between silat and Hinduism are to be found especially in the particular martial arts practices in Bali. To a lesser degree a relationship with Buddhist practices can be examined, at least historically, in the context

---

* *Kuntao* typically refers to martial arts practiced by Chinese overseas communities in Southeast Asia, especially in Malaysia, Indonesia, and parts of the Philippines. In many places it has adapted elements of local martial arts styles into its repertoire and in turn it also influenced local traditions.

of the formation of the Sumatran Srivijaya Empire, and probably beyond.

And last, very little research has so far covered Christian minorities such as the Batak in Sumatra, and their particular types of silat.

The interrelationship of martial arts with spiritual and religious practices in Indonesia and Malaysia is multidimensional and complex. It intricately weaves silat into many layers of *adat* (local customs and traditions), giving silat a vital role in the social and cultural fabric that goes far beyond its function as a means for self-defense. I would venture to generalize that this connection to the local adat is most strongly felt in rural or village settings and enforced within their small independent schools. Here, silat has become an outward expression of cultural and regional identity, reflecting particular local circumstances, spiritual beliefs, and local history.

Strong connections to local customs and traditions notwithstanding, there is also a contrary trend found in Indonesia and Malaysia, and that is the formalization and standardization of silat on national and international levels. In particular, this is happening through the establishment of large schools, international, national, and regional organizations, and through the regular practice of large-scale competitions—all of which move silat more into the realm of sports and further away from its spiritual roots. There is a growing dichotomy between standardization on one hand and preservation efforts of regionally distinct styles on the other. Large organizations such as IPSI (Ikatan Pencak Silat Indonesia—Indonesian Pencak Silat Federation—founded in 1949) have historically played a seminal role in this development. Nowadays the standardization and other issues are negotiated under the auspices of the current international PERSILAT organization (founded in 1980). Standardization and the spread of martial arts around the world—primarily to the Netherlands and the United States in the case of silat—are reshaping the traditions, and hybrid forms are becoming more common. These trends can be seen all across Southeast Asia to varying degrees. In the case of silat, hybridization in the international context as well as on the local level among various regional styles and between silat and kuntao is a topic that certainly warrants further exploration by practitioners and experts in these martial traditions.

Another aspect that deserves further study is the connection of martial arts to other arts, especially dance, music, and theater. Martial arts elements are often used in dramatic performances that feature fighting scenes, such as in Thai *Khon* dance-drama, Sumatran *Randai*, Javanese *Ketoprak*, Philippine *Komedya*, and others. Certainly many of the martial arts have a strong performative quality in and of themselves, and are often publicly presented and appreciated for their aesthetic beauty and sophistication. Comparisons between the performance aspects of Southeast Asian martial arts and other martial dance forms would provide valuable insights into some of their shared roots, movement repertoire, and aesthetics. This in turn can provide practical information on the value of martial arts for the training of dancers and actors within specific performance genres and even beyond the particular genres. This has been done in Indian Kalaripayattu and West Sumatran *silek*, but many more styles remain to be examined.

WILLEM REEDERS (1917–1990) WAS A PIONEER IN BRINGING KUNTAO-SILAT TO THE U.S. ABOVE: HE DEFENDS AGAINST RAY CUNNINGHAM AND ROBERT SERVIDEO IN ERIE, PA, 1960S. RIGHT: REEDERS NEXT TO RICHARD LOPEZ, ONE OF HIS EARLIEST STUDENTS.

*Photographs courtesy of Richard Lopez*

# practical applications

> "It is easier to lead men to combat, stirring up their passion, than to restrain them and direct them toward the patient labour of peace."
>
> ~ Andre Gide (1869-1951)

# Classical Taekwondo

Manuel E. Adrogué, M.A., J.D.*

I have chosen the techniques shown in this article because they represent our system fairly well and I know that, if they fit the situation, they can be used effectively for self-defense. They are not for everyone and need a decent amount of practice. My personal comfort with them comes from the following:

❶ the repetition of Taekwondo basic motions (as found in patterns and fundamental drills) performed with attention to mechanical detail,
❷ the "anatomical weapons" awareness and confidence built by methodically striking hard objects, and
❸ dedicated practice of kicking skills in accordance with the standards set forth by Korean stylists during the 1970s and 80s.

Such basic techniques should follow the idea of generating power using body mass and maximum acceleration of the striking tool upon impact. This demands keeping the body relaxed (especially shoulders and hips), using some (reduced) winding-up motion, and unleashing the power into the target. Winding up is the way to break the inertia by a movement to activate and liberate the center of gravity from its resting state, initiating a sequential chain from the axis (spine) to the limbs as body segments join while the attacking tool increases in acceleration. The windup would be inadmissible in a competition facing a fast, trained, and attentive opponent; for that reason, training to score points focuses on quick motions that should not be detected in their initial state. This is quite different form training for real combat where attention to the final acceleration of techniques prevails over being fast in the initial phase.

Two images may help for practicing. First, hands and feet should be considered rocks swung around the torso; second, arms and legs should be like the ropes of King David's slingshot. Imagine your technique progressively gaining momentum as a sea wave, to fall down into your helpless opponent. The speed of the flying rock and the relaxed downfall of the wave should inspire us. Besides power generation, adequate transfer (application) to the target is crucial.

---

* Editor's note: There are various ways of spelling the name of this martial art, e.g., *Taekwondo, Tae Kwon Do,* and *Taekwon-do.* These differences are based mainly on the politics of organizations. Although Mr. Adrogué prefers the spelling as "Taekwon-Do," we are utilizing our publishing house style, which is based on linguistics.

Taekwondo provides a broad array of techniques using different anatomical weapons of varied paths, lengths, directions, and targets. These may be used in diverse postures so that someone who has mastered the system may, without assuming any preparation or stance, effortlessly deliver a decisive blow to an available target placed at any angle within a certain range of motion. The higher the level of expertise, the shorter the distance needed for issuing a powerful strike.

My primary sources for these concepts were my Moo Duk Kwan and ITF teachers, combined with a talent to analyze and synthesize seemingly opposite ideas. This reverse-engineering approach took me back to the strong Shotokan style and agile Korean kicking. I then focused on General Choi Hong Hi's sine wave theory and body mechanics. All this helped me to understand and become faster to the point where I was being driven by instinct. My thirst for technology on striking power was quite serious, since I only weigh 62 kilos (about 136 lbs).

In a few real-life scenarios, I had previously resorted to the surprise element, weak spots (i.e., the groin), and positioning strategy. Although they had helped me to stay safe, raw striking power put me—and can put anyone—into a completely different league in terms of self-assurance and sense of protection.

Steve Pearlman and Tim Larkin have written about physical martial arts principles and ways to face violence in real-life scenarios. I recommend their work. My personal suggestion is to avoid engaging in violence if at all possible, but if unavoidable, one should take command of the situation, being the first to start the action and releasing a chain of attacks until the situation is terminated.

Martial arts training typically involves an exchange of attacks and defenses among students. Sparring or drills are a form of physical conversation, a relationship using the common language of a system's syllabus and codes. That is great for skill, coordination, and personal improvement, but may lead to dangerous misconceptions. When your life is at stake, there is no contest, no counter technique, no protocol, no dialogue. It is a monologue in which you grab the microphone until you get to say the last word and leave. Alive.

Classical Taekwondo provides many of the tools necessary for survival, but the ability to use them depends exclusively on the decision of each student. We must assume personal responsibility on conditioning mind and body, on gaining accuracy and power, and on investigating the conditions that make techniques work. The true martial artist is both an obedient student who practices what he or she is told, no matter how difficult the teacher's ideas may be to understand (time will clarify), and a skeptical, creative observer who puts everything in doubt. Those two wheels, motored by perseverance, will take the martial artist far in an unforgettable journey.

**Technique 1**

1a) Adrogué is grabbed by his lapel, close to a wall. 1b) He executes an upward ridge-hand strike to the attacker's genitals. 1c) As the attacker bends forward, Adrogué pulls his head into a right upset punch (Hwarang #5). 1d) The attacker stumbles back and Adrogué jump-spins clockwise into the air. 1e) The side kick connects to the face (Yon Gae #44). 1f) The attacker falls backward to the pavement and is no longer a threat.

*Note: Korean names reference motions in Taekwondo patterns.*

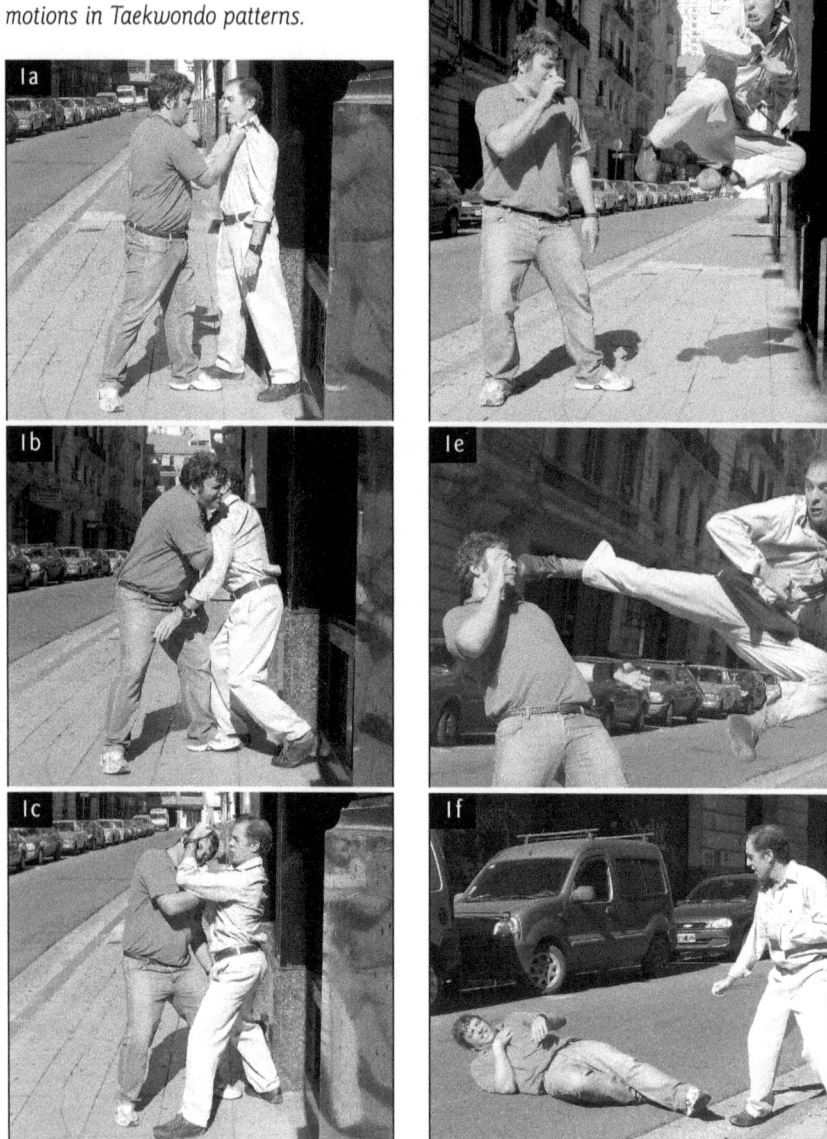

Attacker: Pablo Mayou
Photos by: Leonardo Di Lecce and Alejandro Novas

### Technique 2

**2a)** An unexpected attacker rushes forward. **2b)** Using his inertia, Adrogué crushes the attacker's ribs with a sliding straight punch while controlling his arm (Sam Il #29). **2c)** Adrogué steps in with his right foot to control the attacker's center, rotating the attacker's right hand into an outward wristlock while executing a hammer fist to the face. **2d)** As Adrogué turns counterclockwise, the wristlock and the vacuum generated by his left foot lead the attacker headfirst into the wall. **2e)** To prevent him from recovering, Adrogué's final action is a stomp to the side of his leg to break the knee and ankle.

Asian Martial Arts • Practical Applications

# Iaido and Judo

Peter Boylan, M.A.

The confident posture and cautious awareness developed from training are the most effective self-defense methods I have learned in martial arts. They are more effective than the individual techniques specific to some discrete hypothetical circumstances learned in the normal course of training. I use this posture and awareness every day, in all of my interactions. These techniques have helped me avoid using the specific tactics I study in Kodokan judo, Shinto Hatakage-ryu iaido (sword), and Shinto Muso-ryu jodo (short staff).

The core of martial art practice is self-development, both physical and mental. I can't think of anything that focuses more purely on this than *Mae*, the first kata of Shinto Hatakage-ryu Iai Heiho, which I learned while training with Kiyama Hiroshi in Shiga, Japan. The characteristics of Mae are very similar to other beginning iaido katas: Mae is very limited in movement, allowing students to focus on developing proper posture, proper movement, and a good sense of awareness as they practice.

The practitioner draws, cutting across the opponent's eyes. He then drives forward, raises the sword above his head, and does a large cut down into the assailant. The trick is to maintain good posture and balance while performing the kata. Mae is the simplest kata in the system, the foundation of everything else that follows in Shinto Hatakage-ryu. The student learns to move with a strong upright posture, maintaining a solid foundation and clear, focused external awareness. This seemingly simple kata is incredibly difficult for students to do properly, but once stance, movement, and awareness are developed, these principles begin to express themselves in the student in all areas of activity, not just during sword-drawing practice. This is the real goal of the kata. The student gains in the fundamentals of movement and awareness that are most important in preventing situations that may require the further use of discrete techniques, such as joint locks, strikes, or throws. People who move well and have a solid foundation naturally have a strong, confident-looking posture and good awareness, thus failing the predator's test of looking like vulnerable prey. The ones who have successfully defended themselves are those who aren't attacked. This is the best kind of self-defense—where you don't even know you've defended yourself because nothing happened.

Since most violence is actually committed by people with whom we are familiar, I thought I would include one technique that can potentially be used by a woman against an annoying acquaintance or relative. The technique is a variation on the Kodokan judo hip throw *ogoshi* ("major hip"). This was one of the first techniques I learned in my college judo class. The situation of the kata assumes that the woman is being pressured by someone who is not taking "no" for an answer. In this variation, the assault is coming from someone who is well known to the woman, someone who can approach her and pressure her seemingly without threat of violence. The familiar assailant can get close and even put his arm around the woman's shoulders without threatening her, but still pressures her for something.

*ogoshi*

The point where the assailant has his arm around the woman's shoulders, feeling like he's in control, perhaps even reaching out and taking her hand, is actually the end of his control. The woman can smile agreeably, put her arm around his waist, squeeze his hand tight, shift her hip across in front of him, and throw him over her hip to the ground.

This is a nice technique that is strong but flexible. Depending on how threatened the woman feels, she can throw the man gently to the floor, or she can accelerate him and smash him into the ground. It's her choice because she is in control. The individual's ability to choose the level of force involved makes this major hip throw variation a good option. The technique is also a great surprise to the man!

A week after learning the major hip throw variation in a beginning college judo class, a student came running into class yelling, "It works! It works!" With some hesitation, my teacher asked, "What works?" The student said, "The throw you showed us last week. I was at a dance and my date started getting fresh, so I stepped in and threw him!"

**Technique 1: Iai Kata**

This is the first kata students learn, and all the fundamentals of moving with good posture are contained in it. In the first photo (1a), there is good, solid posture at the start. This posture is maintained through the initial draw and cut to the opponent's face (1b), and maintained through the last cut and beyond, even during the cleaning and sheathing of the sword (1c).

Right:
Hana Mitsusada-Boylan
demonstrating this
effective throw.

*Photography by
Mark Richard Frye*

**Technique 2: Judo Kata**

When someone pushes himself on a woman (**2a**) and he doesn't take "Go away" for an answer, she can use as little or as much force as needed. She can seem to go along with him by slipping her arm around his back and holding his hand as she slips her hip across in front of him (**2b**). Then with a small lift of her legs, she can throw him over her hips (**2c**).

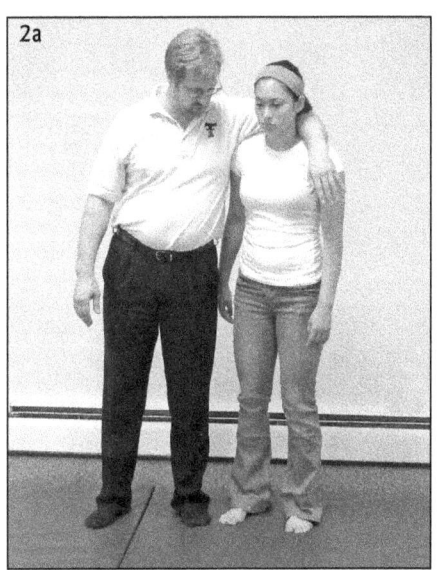

# Sinmoo Hapkido

Sean Bradley, N.D., E.A.M.P.

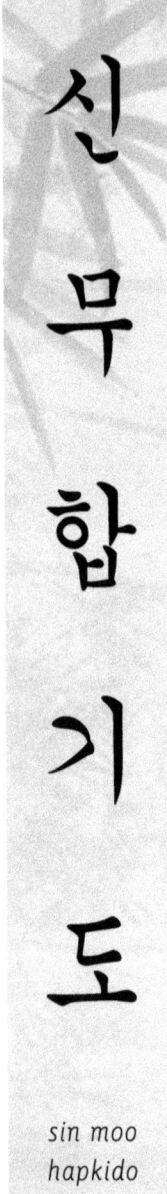

sin moo hapkido

### Where I Learned These Techniques

The basic armbar and the high-section roundhouse kick represent two of the foundational techniques that demonstrate important principles of body mechanics, movement, and technical detail imperative to the art of Sinmoo Hapkido as taught by Dojunim Ji Han-Jae.* I was introduced to both of these techniques in my first class with Dojunim Ji in New Jersey, but have been forced to constantly refine them as I continue to train and better understand the art.

### Memorable Incidents Involving These Techniques

The first time Dojunim Ji applied the basic arm bar to me was during my first class with him. I grabbed his wrist and in an instant my face was nearly smashed into the floor. I felt as though my elbow was ripped apart and my wrist was about to explode. The pain was excruciating and there was nothing I could do to fight it.

As for the high-section roundhouse kick, I remember drilling this kick for hours at various times as Dojunim Ji constantly adjusted my footwork, body position, and rhythm of movement. The roundhouse kick is the seventh of the twenty-five basic kicks of Sinmoo Hapkido, and is one of the kicks that give students the most trouble in the beginning. Unfortunately, the most memorable aspect of this technique involves the numerous injuries I have seen people suffer from attempting this kick. Too often, rather than listen to the details of the technique and approach it

---

\* *Dojunim* is the honorary title for Ji Han-Jae as the founder of the Korean martial art of Sinmoo Hapkido. Ji is also considered by many to be the founder of modern Hapkido.

as a completely new kick, students attempt to perform another style of roundhouse kick, but reach one hand toward the floor, since that is the most obvious feature of how this kick is different. Unfortunately, without all the details, I've seen far too many people drop to the floor grasping a strained hamstring as they mix opposing mechanics.

**Tips on Practicing These Techniques**

For the basic armbar, the most important tip is not to muscle through the technique, but to use your whole body. It is easy to apply a joint lock to a cooperative opponent, but to apply this technique effectively, you must first unbalance the attacker with the initial step and drop of the body. The side step and drop not only allow you to unbalance the attacker, but also bring the hand to your own midline so you are able to move using your whole body effectively. Pivot the feet and lean forward slightly as you rotate your hips to lock the attacker's arm straight. Continue to control his balance by keeping him on his heels.

It is also important to have the proper graduated handgrip, and to pin the hand to your chest on application so as not to rely on strength, but let body mechanics do the work. Use your body, and also apply leverage to the attacker's thumb to aid in creating some pain compliance, but, more important, keep his arm straight.

The high-section roundhouse kick exists in many forms in many different styles but is unique in its application in Sinmoo Hapkido. This kick utilizes the top of the instep at the ankle or the shin to strike the temple or neck area. The head and torso deliberately drop low in order to allow the leg to go up and kick higher than normal flexibility may allow. Additionally, this motion also drops the head out of the way of a potential strike, and the palm of the hand touches the floor to provide additional balance and push to return to an upright position.

Though most people notice the hand touching the ground and point to this as the major distinguishing factor, it is only a small aspect that sets this technique apart. Dropping the head to allow the leg to get higher without relying solely on flexibility is an important part of performing this kick correctly, but stepping on a forty-five-degree angle and allowing the body to fold at nearly a ninety-degree angle are imperative to ensure optimal power and also decrease the stress on the low back. The regular rhythm is a four-step count that allows the body to move fluidly in a rocking motion that enables the kick to act as a whip.

### Technique 1: Basic Armbar

1a) Spread the fingers of the hand being grabbed creating tension and expanding the tendons of the wrist. 1b) Take a small side step to the right with the right foot and sink straight down by bending the knees. The right hand moves below the grabbing hand to the outside and then lifts straight, using the legs to stand up. The left hand reaches across and grabs the hypothenar eminence of the attacker's left hand, using the little, ring, and middle fingers to wrap around the meat of the hand below the little finger. The index finger remains straight and pointed. Create a tight seal across the back of the hand by placing the thumb pad at the base of the thumb knuckle. Force should be applied to lock the wrist in a bent position. 1c) With your left hand, pull the attacker's hand to your chest as the right hand applies pressure forward against his thumb. 1d) The left foot pivots to the outside, keeping the attacker's hand to the chest and moving the right hand up to three finger widths above the elbow in a tense, active hand position. 1e) Step forward with the right foot as you apply downward pressure just above the wrist to execute the armbar.

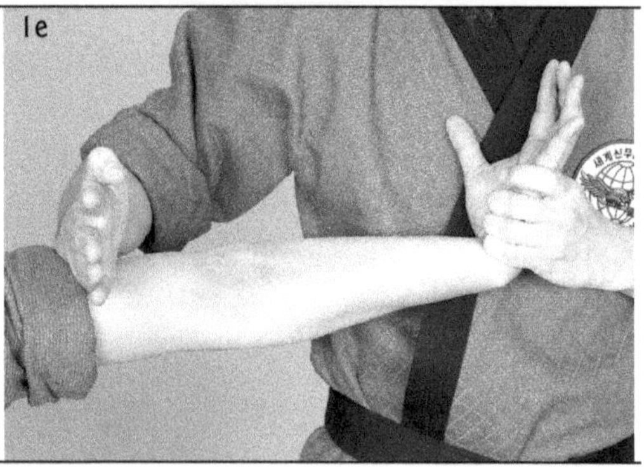

### Technique 2: High-Section Roundhouse Kick

**2a)** Start in a neutral position. **2b)** Step on a forty-five-degree angle to the left. **2c)** The body bends at the waist and the left shoulder begins to drop toward the floor.

### Acknowledgement

Warm thanks to Tiffany Tong for the photography and to Alex Mark for helping demonstrate.

**2d)** The right knee lifts up and begins to swing in a circular motion to the inside. The left foot pivots slightly on the ball of the foot as the right hip pushes forward and the knee snaps the right foot forward in a whiplike motion. As the foot reaches maximum extension, the left palm touches the floor while the body bends in almost an "L" shape **(side view 2e)**. The left hand pushes the torso up as the right foot snaps back at the knee and pulls downward toward the floor. The left foot pivots, and when the right foot steps down, the left then steps back to return to the neutral standing posture.

# Clinch Fighting, Chinese Style

Jake Burroughs

Clinch work is often overlooked or altogether neglected in many traditional Chinese martial arts academies. Though prevalent in *Shuaijiao* (Chinese wrestling), many other schools simply do not incorporate the clinch range into their martial curriculum. Here in my farewell article for the *Journal of Asian Martial Arts*, I wish to share two takedowns from the clinch range, one ideal for when you have the single high-collar tie, and the other illustrating what to do if your opponent has the high-collar tie. Though technically these techniques are derived from Xingyiquan and Six Harmonies Praying Mantis boxing, variations can be found throughout the martial spectrum, and the principles will span geographic origins.

I encourage my students to rely on principles, and with this article it is imperative that the student understands what Tim Cartmell has coined the "dead angle"—essentially being the attack angle where an individual's base is weakest. Assuming a natural shoulder-width stance, draw a line between your ankles. From the midpoint 90 degrees both forward and back, you will find your two dead angles. Think about having a third leg, much like a tri-pod. The dead angle is what you are trying to exploit with your opponent, and conversely what you are constantly trying to hide from your counterpart.

> **"Gravity doesn't lie, and the ground never misses."**
> — Tim Cartmell, on the efficacy of throws and takedowns in self-defense situations

The first technique is straight from the two-person set called the Five Flower Cannon (*wu hua pao*), common in almost all Xingyi systems. Traditionally, one would strike to bridge the gap and then execute this foot sweep, but here I am showing it from clinch range if my opponent has a high-collar tie (important note: if he has a "full plum," or both hands breaking down my posture, *this will not work!*). It is crucial that I keep control of his free hand while breaking his grip and driving his arm into his body, eliciting a classic push-pull response. When I press into him, threatening his posture, he settles his base and pushes back, and it is at that precise moment I step back and sweep out his foot, simultaneously pulling his arm to his rear dead angle. Sensitivity to the subtle weight shift in your opponent's body is critical for executing this properly, but anyone of any build can do this sweep, and it completely catches your partner off guard.

The second technique is drawn from Six Harmonies Praying Mantis, but can be found as "neck mopping" in Shuaijiao, maintains the principles of *pi quan* (downward energy) from Xingyi, and is often seen as an application of the single- palm change in Bagua. This time we have the high single-collar tie on our opponent, and once again it is important that I keep control of his free hand, both to avoid being struck and to manipulate his structure.

Pulling with my right arm on the base of his skull (*not* the neck), I sidestep to the left a bit and slide my right foot over and back. By pulling into his forward dead angle he is forced to step with his left leg, which squares his body to mine. To execute the takedown, I simply step with my lead leg into his center, driving with my right arm over and down. I can assist my right arm by tapping his right knee to ensure he does not step out.

I have fond memories of training one on one with Mr. Hu, my mantis teacher, in his living room, where he would use this technique on me over and over again, throwing me onto the couch! No mats, no training space, simply the hardwood floor and the couch pushed a few inches "out of the way." This was one of his favorite takedowns, and a living embodiment of martial arts: he was 120 pounds soaking wet, but I have seen him throw three-hundred-pound Texans with this simple takedown, all based on leverage and technical skill, not size and strength!

## Acknowledgements
Thanks to Mike Robinson for help in the photographs. Thanks to Northwest Jiu Jitsu Academy for letting us use the space for the photo shoot. Big thanks to Dana at DKB Images for the professional photography.

I also want to thank the *Journal of Asian Martial Arts*, and more specifically Michael DeMarco, for giving so much to the community of martial scholars and researchers and never once asking for anything in return. It saddens me to see you go, but I am proud to have been a part of your journey.

## Technique 1: Push-Pull Sweep

**1a)** Mike has a single high-collar tie on Jake (note the proper placement of the hand on the base of the skull, not the neck), so Jake quickly secures Mike's free hand to protect against strikes and to prevent him from gaining an even more superior position.

**1b)** As Jake switches his base by stepping with his left foot behind Mike's lead leg, he simultaneously presses down and in on Mike's right arm at the crease in the elbow (think of driving his elbow to his opposite foot).

**1c)** Here Jake presses into Mike, causing him to push back. Notice how Jake is hooking his left foot and pressing with his left leg into Mike's right leg. Also note how Mike's right elbow is being driven into his center.

**1d–f)** Perfecting the timing here can be tricky, but as Mike shifts his weight forward Jake takes advantage by stepping back with his right foot and sweeping Mike's lead leg. Notice how Jake sweeps in the direction of Mike's toes, and how Jake is pulling Mikes' right arm back toward his dead angle.

1a

1b

1c

## Technique 2: Neck Mopping

**2a)** In this situation Jake has the high-collar tie. Again note the hand on the base of Mike's skull, and the importance of controlling Mike's free hand.

**2b)** Taking a small step with his left foot, Jake pulls Mike into his front dead angle forcing Mike to step with his left foot.

**2c–d)** Jake drives into Mike's center by stepping with his lead leg, tapping his knee with the left arm, simultaneously driving his right arm over and down into Mike's dead angle.

**2e)** Jake finishes by driving through his opponent.

Asian Martial Arts • Practical Applications

# Wing Chun

Joyotpaul "Joy" Chaudhuri, Ph.D.

## Where I Learned These Techniques

Augustine Fong was a top student of Ho Kamming of Macao, who studied for many years with Ip Man (1893–1972), the central figure in the spreading of Wing Chun (*Yong Chun*). I began studying at Fong's Wing Chun Academy in Tucson in 1976. To serious students, Fong teaches the complete art: its principles, concepts, forms, wooden dummy, weapons, hands-on practice, foundation-based techniques, and interactive application and adjustment to varying situations. Stability, mobility, sharp timing, spontaneous and reflexive action, relatively squared body, double handedness, understanding lines and angles, and coordinated usage of the entire body rather than excessive muscle tension are all features of good teaching and learning of the style.

Wing Chun has many techniques, but actual situations and opponents can vary so much that Wing Chun does not depend on fixed answers to fixed attacks. A situation can be handled in a variety of ways. Doing lots of Wing Chun tends to develop natural and spontaneous responses. But all techniques emerge from three fundamental arm positions: wing (*bong*), control (*fook*), and spreading (*tan*). These positionings allow one to protect the center line emerging from one's own body, particularly the central axis, from different directions and planes. Ideally, the positions also allow power to be directed to the other person's axis.

The two techniques or motions chosen for this article are the slapping-spreading combination (*pak-tan*), and the pulling-hitting combination (*lop-da*). To be successful with both—in addition to the timing practice of various kinds of sticky hands—it's important to master the stability of the Wing Chun stance and learning how to turn and step. The hand structures have to be integrated with the structures of the upper and lower body, connected by controlling the center point complex of the body (*dantian*). In Wing Chun structures, geometry plays a role. Triangles and their adjustment to circles are important.

## Memorable Incidences

Years ago I used the slapping-spreading combination in controlling a powerful punch thrown by a burly attacker in a bus station. And I used it in moving in on a skilled kenpo person kicking at my head. With footwork I used the pulling-hitting combination in neutralizing a visiting grappler's attempt to take me down. These and other empirical experiences helped me to understand the effectiveness of learning good Wing Chun.

**Tips on Practice**

The development of the slapping-spreading combination requires the index fingers of the slapping and spreading hands to meet at the apex of a triangle, with both elbows forming the other two points. The elbows are sunk, but springy and strong. Upon or near contact, the slapping and spreading hands can spread to adjust to the incoming force while still using an adapted triangular formation. Understanding the range of the work and limits of the springing and appropriate circling qualities of all the joints (particularly the elbows, wrists, and knees) is important. My partner, Joshua Santobianco, is a powerful striker and a well-trained grappler who is well versed in Wing Chun. In the photographs taken by Dana Albert, I am shown adjusting the slapping-spreading combination to control the force of Joshua's strike.

The development of the pulling-hitting combination also involves the coordination of the *lop* (a grabbing motion) with the protective hand (*wu sao*). Again, the elbows help create a triangular formation of the forearms and hands. The grabbing motion can be used effectively in close-quarter control of the opponent at the point of contact: forearm, shoulder, and head are examples. In the photo (2b), I am shown controlling Josh's left-hand strike with a wing hand (*bong*) and a protective hand. The protective hand quickly turns into a grab (2c) by sinking the elbow, and the wing arm turns into a strike by swiveling the elbow. The two hands need to work together.

In using these two techniques, basic Wing Chun principles apply. Maintain your own structural balance, disturb the other person's, and control the center line connecting the axis of your structure with that of your opponent.

In good Wing Chun, if you can control your own balance—and your opponent's—you can do whatever you intend, including stopping an attack, striking, kicking, breaking, or throwing. With good practice, the two techniques discussed can perform all these functions. The final moves of each sequence (1e and 2e) illustrate the possibilities in controlling and breaking structures through the use of Wing Chun.

Following pages: Chaudhuri's partner in action shots is Joshua Santobianco.

*Photography by Dana Albert.*

## TECHNIQUE 1: Pak-tan Combination

1a) Josh strikes; Joy readies to block with a left slapping hand and right spreading hand combination. 1b) Stepping in, Joy uses a left slapping with a right palm-up protective motion. 1c) The slapping palm controls Josh's structure via his elbow, and Joy's right executes a palm-up neck strike. 1d) Joy's right hand controls Josh while he strikes with his left palm down. 1e) Joy's left leg moves in to control Josh's knee, getting ready for a fast torquing and throwing Josh down to the ground.

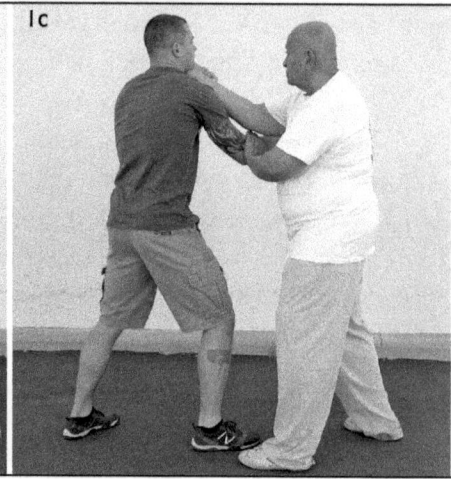

## TECHNIQUE 2: Lop-da Combination

**2a)** Josh begins to strike. Joy prepares to make contact with his right wing forearm and positions a protective left hand. **2b)** Joy deflects and controls with the wing arm's contact point. **2c)** Shifting, Joy's protective hand grabs the wrist to control Josh and simultaneously chops Josh's neck with the right hand. **2d)** Joy folds Josh's left arm, trapping both hands while pulling his head down, breaking his structure and balance. **2e)** Joy continues to torque and knees Josh.

# Kuntao, Silat

Philip H. J. Davies, Ph.D.

> From the flower [form] comes the fruit [applications];
> From the fruit [applications] comes the kernel [principles].
> — *Silat aphorism*

## Kuntao, Silat, and Gongfu

In recent years, Pencak Silat has acquired a level of visibility and awareness in the Western martial arts community that it had not previously enjoyed. Silat is not, however, the only martial arts tradition of the Indo-Malay archipelago. The next most prominent tradition is that of *kuntao*, nowadays rendered in the common Malay and Indonesian spelling scheme as *kuntau*. Kuntao is a loan word from Fujian Chinese (specifically the Southern Min or "Amoy" dialect). In its native language, kuntao is a generic term for martial arts, much like *wushu* or *gongfu* in Mandarin. In Indonesian, the term is most commonly employed to signify arts that combine Chinese and Indonesian arts, techniques, principles, and training regimens. "Kuntao" is, however, a somewhat volatile identity because once the synthesis occurs, the resulting art is no longer compatible with strict Chinese tradition and typically the system becomes absorbed within the silat community and conventions of practice within a couple of generations.

## Tiger-Style Kuntao

Since 1981 I have trained primarily in the art of Kuntao Matjan, or Tiger-style kuntao, brought to the West by the late Paatje Carel Faulhaber and still taught in Canada by his closest student, Paatje Richard Kudding. Both being of culturally marginal Dutch-Indonesian heritage, the practice of a culturally marginal art was probably less of a challenge than for ethnic Chinese or *pribumi* Indonesians, for whom an art and its ethnic heritage are more integrally bound. Unfortunately, Faulhaber passed away unexpectedly from a brief, severe illness in 1974, barely fifty years old and before he could pass on a detailed account of his system to his students.

Consequently, a number of practitioners in the tradition have made efforts to trace their art's origins, starting with the late Harry de Spa in the 1990s. He interviewed a contemporary and close friend of Faulhaber's called Henk Andersen, who recalled Faulhaber describing his art as based largely on a Chinese tiger-boxing system learned from a "half-blind," presumably one-eyed, ethnic Chinese teacher during Faulhaber's childhood in Semarang in northern Central Java during the 1930s (de Spa, 1996 1997a, 1997b). In 2003 I undertook a research trip to Semarang, ably assisted by the anthropologist Lee Wilson, where we interviewed a senior master of Golden Eagle (*Garuda Mas*) Kuntao called Edhi Chandera. According to Chandera, there has only ever been one Chinese master in the Semarang area who had only one eye, Liem Tjoei Kang (Davies & Wilson, 2003a, 2003b). Although Liem is today remembered chiefly as a leading practitioner of Five Ancestors Gongfu, he learned this system from his uncle, Lo Ban Teng (Lu Wanding 盧万定), after settling in Indonesia (Davies & Wilson, 2003a; Tjoa, 1959). Liem arrived already an accomplished practitioner, and Chandera was adamant that his original teaching include both Fujian Crane and Fujian Tiger styles. Thus it seems most likely that Faulhaber studied Fujian Tiger Boxing from Liem Tjoei Kang during the 1930s when, according to recollections of one of his Dutch-Indo contemporaries in Semarang, he was given to playing truant from school to go and train with Liem and his Chinese students.

Less is known of the silat source or sources of Faulhaber's art. We know from his personal record in the Dutch national archive (den Hague, 1974) that he spent time not only in Semarang but also Palembang in Sumatra, as well as Belitang, Martapura, and Sorong in what is now Irian Jaya (New Guinea), and reportedly also Jakarta (then called Batavia). Paatje Richard recalls Faulhaber speaking of a *dukun*, or traditional Indonesian spiritualist and healer who taught him. From my time spent studying silat in Southeast Asia many movements appear in the system that are reminiscent of the Javanese varieties of Tiger-style silat one encounters in both Sundanese and Bugis traditions. Whatever the specific influences, the result is a closely fused synthesis of the two traditions that results in a coherent, effective art in its own right.

**Acknowledgement:** Much appreciation to David White for help demonstrating the technical section and to Neelufer Jauffur as photographer.

---

**References**
Davies, P. and Wilson, L. (2003a). Interview with Edhi Chandera. Semarang, 9 September.
Davies, P. and Wilson, L. (2003b). Interview with Edhi Chandera. Semarang, 10 September.
De Spa, H. (1996, 19 November). Notes interview with Paatje Henk Andersen. Arnhem.
De Spa, H. (1997a). E-mail correspondence with PHJ Davies, July 6.
De Spa, H. (1997b). E-mail correspondence with PHJ Davies, July 8.
Den Hague. (1974, 29 July). Personal record of Carel Faulhaber.
Tjoa, Khek Kjong [Kiong]. (1959, 7 February). "'Malaikat Berwajah Putih' dari Siauw Lim Ho Yang Pei," *Harian Star Weekly*.

## Technique 1

1a) This sequence is one of the short, silat-style forms called *jalan kaki*, or "walking" techniques. This example is typical of Sundanese Tiger style.
1b) Retreat and compound block.
1c) Knee kick.
1d) Step in, pulling the opponent; grab the back of his head.

1e) Elbow strike. 1f) Rising knee strike. 1g) Set up sweep. 1h) Sweep. 1i) Finishing punch.

---

## Technique 2

2a) A squatting horse with a turn-the-wheel block was demonstrated by Edhi Chandera during an interview as distinctive to Liem's Tiger style. This version occurs in four of Faulhaber's long Chinese-style forms or *kembang*. 2b) Step in circle block.
2c) Squatting horse, drag down and trap the arm. 2d) Rise with tiger's claw.

# Chen Taijiquan

David Gaffney, B.A.

**Chen Village Style: Using Soft to Neutralize and Hard to Emit**

Chen Wangting created a new kind of martial art almost four hundred years ago in Chen Village. Chen Taijiquan has been refined and passed on through generations of village boxers up to the present day. An important concept lying at the heart of its devastating fighting skills is the use of softness to change and neutralize an attack, followed by hardness to emit force at the point when an opponent's position has become compromised. Since the mid-1990s—training with Chen Xiaowang, gatekeeper of the family style, and with his younger brother, Chen Xiaoxing, head of the Chenjiagou Taijiquan School—I've come to realize the breadth of this principle.

In the school, training is intense and physically very demanding, as befits one of China's most traditional martial arts. While Chen Taijiquan includes many kicks and strikes within its arsenal, in essence it is a close-range throwing and grappling system. The realities of combat necessitate that a practitioner be well versed and comfortable during close-quarter fighting. The system is renowned for its joint locking, throwing, and takedowns—all built upon its unique use of spiraling energy. It is this "silk reeling" quality that enables a skilled practitioner to use the strength of an antagonist against himself.

Chen Xiaowang (2011) explains: "When somebody comes with force we use the soft neutralizing method to change the direction of the incoming force. The opponent attacks our centerline and we change the direction and take the momentum out of his force. That is what is called *rou hua* (pliant neutralizing). At the moment that the opponent loses his balance we use our *gang jin* [hard power] to attack the most appropriate part of his body and that is what is called *rou hua gang fa*."

**Chen Zhaochi Defeats a Bandit**

Training applications with a teacher like Chen Xiaowang is a painful experience. He is adamant that you must experience the real technique if you are to really understand it and have confidence in the method. This confidence is vital if a Taijiquan practitioner is to meet a true attack with softness and without hesitation. Chen Xiaowang recounted the story of how Chen Zhaochi

(1928–1981) used the principle of "neutralizing before returning force" to deadly effect when he was suddenly ambushed on a remote mountain path: "A bandit was hiding in a tree with a stick with the intention of attacking him when he passed. Before the stick could make contact, Zhaochi instinctively reacted by intercepting and then returning the weapon, striking the bandit on the head and killing him" (2008: 43). To his way of thinking, kicking and punching represent a relatively low level of martial skill compared to the internalized ability to instantaneously blend with a sudden violent and unexpected attack, in the process turning it back upon the person who launched the attack.

### Practice Tips

- As an opponent attacks, it is crucial to remain balanced and centered. In the instant that contact is made, one must be able to assess the attack's speed, direction, strength, and quality. This is referred to as "listening" and "discerning" energy. During this process, one must make constant subtle changes to the body's posture, maintaining the center while following the direction of the incoming force.
- Don't neutralize and only then think of what to do next. In the process of neutralizing, one should be storing energy to instantly attack once the incoming force is dissipated. Chen Xiaowang (2011) says, "This is very effective because as he is losing his balance, I am storing my strength." While you are neutralizing, the aim of the practitioner is not to think of hitting the opponent; first defuse the incoming force. Placing too much emphasis on hardness during push-hands is a common error and represents a loss of principle.
- Following and exploiting an opponent's strength is the skill of spotting the right opportunity to take advantage of his position when it is compromised. As an opponent executes his attack, the aim is to follow the direction of his movement and, at the point when he is uncomfortable and in a disadvantageous position, to then enter and attack. As the opponent realizes his technique is not going to work, he naturally tries to change his movement. As he begins to go back after failing with an attack, a person with good push-hands ability just adds a little of his own strength to take advantage of the situation. In Taijiquan parlance this is known as borrowing strength.

---

**References**
Chen X.W. (2008). *Chen Family Taijiquan*. Henan: People's Sports Publishing Company.
Chen X.W. (2011). *Secrets of Taiji: Taijiquan tuishou* (episode 8). Beijing: China Central Television, CTV5, Sports Channel.

## Technique 1

**1a)** Chen Xiaowang and the author practicing forward- and backward-stepping push-hands.

**1b)** As Chen pushes forward, David follows the movement and neutralizes the attack with diverting force.

**1c–d)** When the force is dissipated, Chen returns in a smooth circular motion to apply a forceful joint-locking technique.

### Technique 2

**2a–b)** Andrew Hesketh punches toward the author, who diverts the attack.

**2c)** Immediately after the force of Andrew's punch is spent, David attacks with an elbow, pulling Andrew's arm in the opposite direction to increase the effect of the technique.

**2d–e)** Without any stop, David extends his right arm while controlling Andrew's left arm. Finally David applies a tight neck lock, at the same time stepping in close to control Andrew's ability to respond.

# Ryukyu Kempo and Small Circle Jujitsu

Will Higginbotham, B.A.

## Where I Learned These Techniques

As a strong proponent of the value of classical kata practice, I stress that applications for techniques can be derived directly from traditional katas. Further, karate and jujutsu techniques work wonderfully well together to "fill in the gaps" in seeking ways to maintain control of an attacker.

The particular sets of techniques or "flows" presented in this article are variations on—and combinations of—well-known and commonly practiced individual techniques. The reason these sets are among my favorites is that they illustrate the importance of preventing the practitioner from simply "stalling out" after performing a single counter to a given attack.

The first set deals with a takedown to a prone position from a hammerlock, using a finger lock for maximum stability and control. Here I credit Leon Jay (Small Circle Jujitsu) for sharing his expertise in joint manipulation.

The second set involves a series of defenses from a right-left punch combination delivered by a determined assailant. At each step the defender aims to control his opponent and deter further aggression, using force proportionate to the nature and duration of the attack. By aiming blocks and strikes at specific pressure points, the defender hopes to injure or disable the attacking arm, stun the attacker, and finally subdue him altogether by taking him to the ground in a controlled fashion. Here I credit George Dillman (Ryukyu Kempo) for sharing his expertise with pressure-point techniques.

## Memorable Incidents Involving These Techniques

The hammerlock is sometimes taught as a static technique, leaving the defender holding the attacker in a somewhat precarious standing position from which a number of counters and escapes can be performed. A common follow-up is the application of additional torque to the shoulder, forcing the opponent to the prone position on the floor. One problem with this follow-up is that the defender is often forced to slam the opponent downward in order to maintain control. The version presented here shows how the defender can maintain a higher degree of control throughout the encounter.

One of my senior students—sixth dan Anthony Everett—is the agent in charge of training on the national level for the Department of Veterans Affairs. Because of the superior control afforded by the takedown from the hammerlock presented herein, the agency has adopted this particular technique as part of its combatives training in controlling and handcuffing.

The defense for the right-left combination attack is similarly controlled, but equally powerful and adaptable. One sensible goal is to use the minimum force required to prevent the attack and keep oneself safe. This is important for ethical as well as legal reasons. In the sequence illustrating the defense against the right-left punch combination, the defender reacts to protect himself and control the situation with escalating force, making sure the response at each stage is proportionate to the increasing intensity of the attack.

This technique is also highly adaptable. For example, when working this technique with a Muay Thai stylist at a European seminar in 2008, the attacker had the good sense and training to retract his left fist to guard his jaw after I had blocked his second attack. Luckily, force can be easily transferred through a solid object, and I was able to complete the technique perfectly simply by palming the attacker's own guard into the intended target.

### Tips on Practicing These Techniques

In applying the controlled takedown from the hammerlock, the free hand is used to control the shoulder, preventing the opponent from turning counter-clockwise to spin out of the hold. As the right hand slides down and behind the opponent to grasp his fingers, the left hand snakes around the elbow to create a base and prevent a spinning or turning counter to the finger lock. As the defender applies controlled pressure to the fingers, the left hand strokes the carotid sinus to force the opponent to the ground.

In the defense against the right and left punch sequence, the defender begins with a guard position that is intended to be relatively nonthreatening. When the attacker punches, the defender parries and simultaneously "stings" the sensitive points on the inside of the wrist with his other hand, so as to deter any further attack if possible. If the attacker continues with a left punch, the defender clears the parried right punch down and to the side while simultaneously parrying the incoming attack with his rising, right ridge hand. If these two defenses have not ended the confrontation, the defender is now inside the attacker's guard and has a clear shot at neck and head targets. Finally, by cupping the back of the attacker's neck with the right hand while leaving the left hand free, the defender can apply as little or as much force as is needed to take the attacker down and can control his fall to boot.

## Technique 1: Controlled Takedown from the Hammerlock

1a) The defender slaps the opponent's attacking right forearm down with his left palm, then shoots his right hand across and behind the attacker's elbow. 1b) The defender continues around the forearm with his left hand and pulls with his right to rotate the opponent. He "tightens" the hammerlock by stroking the right palm up. 1c) The defender slides his right hand down and behind to grasp his opponent's ring and pinky fingers. His left hand wraps the elbow from inside to prevent twisting out of the finger lock. 1d) Once the finger lock is secure with the right hand alone, the middle finger of the left hand strokes up the sternocleidomastoid muscle, forcing the assailant to fall on his back. The reverse two-finger lock is then used to flip him over on his face, using his left hand to cup his head for safety. 1e) The defender can now base the finger lock with his leg for more intense control while kneeling on the opponent's sciatic nerve to stabilize him.

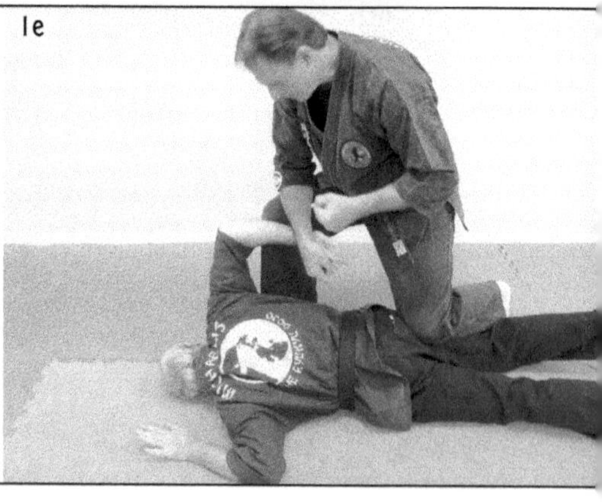

**Technique 2: Escalating Defense from Right and Left Punches**

**2a)** When confronted, the defender assumes a hands-up, palm-open "don't hurt me" type of posture. **2b)** If the attacker strikes, the defender parries down with a left open-palm slap while striking to the inside of the wrist with a right punch. **2c)** If the attack continues with the free left hand, the defender's parrying hand continues its arc to clear the opponent's right arm. The defender's right ridge hand parries up, striking. **2d)** The defender is now inside his attacker's guard and in a position to strike simultaneously to the neck and jaw. **2e)** The defender's right hand snakes around to cup the attacker's neck, while his left hand can press or strike the forehead as needed to subdue the attacker with minimum damage and maximum control.

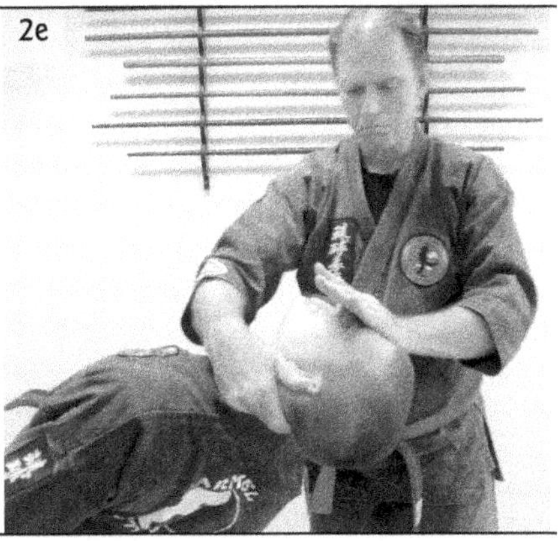

# Baguazhang

Hong Tsehan

### Where I Learned These Techniques

Of course I am biased, but even by others' accounts, my father Hong Yixiang (洪懿祥 1925–1993), was one of the twentieth century's most notable teachers of Chinese martial arts. He gained fame in Taiwan as a fighting master of Xingyi, Bagua, and Taiji, training students who won national tournaments in the 1970s. His skill was made known to the world by Robert W. Smith's pioneering Chinese martial arts books, and *The Way of the Warrior*, BBC's profile about him. His prominence was further spread in Taiwan, the United States and beyond by the many Taiwanese and foreign students he taught, such as Eric Luo, Su Dongcheng, Robert Yu, Mark Griffin, Chris Bates, Marcus Brinkman, and Abi Moriya.

My grandfather wanted his sons to have a well-rounded martial education and invited top teachers as they fled mainland China with the KMT to teach them. Among these teachers were Zhang Zhunfeng (張峻峰) and Chen Panling (陳泮嶺). Both of these teachers saw the potential of my father and uncles and drilled them hard, seeking to prove that local Taiwanese could stand up to the best mainland fighters. This they did. Ultimately, my father and uncles each mastered their own specialties.

The passing on of a martial arts system from a father to his sons is a venerable tradition in China. My brothers and I were schooled intensely by my father and uncles and competed with each other for our father's attention through the training. After his untimely death, we continued to combine our knowledge and train with our uncle, Hong Yimian, until he died.

### Memorable Incidents Involving These Techniques

As engendered in the lineage name—Yizong Cheng School Gao-Style Baguazhang (易宗程派高式八卦掌), brought to Taiwan by Zhang Zhunfeng and passed down by Hong Yixiang (*yizong* meaning essence of change)—recognizes that change is an inherent element of combat between two opponents. Being able to change in response to an opponent, to adapt, is a fundamental skill in Bagua. A higher level of skill encoded into the training sequences is to bring overwhelming change to the opponent, change that attacks his very ability to adapt to it. I coined the term *3D fighting* to describe this. Bagua forms anticipate several responses from the opponent, and to each response Bagua has an answer that leads to further control over the opponent until he is defeated. Typically, this control is established by manipulating the opponent to his very core. Through such techniques as locking up limbs, breaking balance, and blinding, we disrupt his ability to adapt to change.

On one occasion thirty some years ago, I was sparring in the old school with one of the senior students famous for his very mobile and fluid Xingyi style. It was an "ah-ha" moment for me when I was able to get Bagua's indirect stepping and overwhelming change to work for me. We were both suited in the chest protectors designed by my father that allowed heavy contact. My opponent was very mobile and fast, difficult to attack frontally. I circled to his right outside and controlled his right arm, punching repeatedly low and high into his chest. Six blows landed as I drove him back. Finally, he jerked back the arm I had controlled, turning his body into the action and launching a left cross. I was able to adapt to this change, ducking under and parrying his strike over my head, twisting his body, unbalancing him at the core, and shoving him off balance. It was one of those moments that feel like magic as he just sailed away uncontrollably.

**Tips on Practicing the Techniques**

Bagua sequences embrace change, prepare the practitioner for change, and fundamentally target the opponent's capacity to adapt to change. Practice the form alone, then with a partner. A key element is "bridging"—to close the measure with the opponent and make contact with his guard. With a partner, practice making the initial bridging technique from different sides and angles. Learn to make the bridge and follow-up technique quickly and smoothly, keeping in mind that sometimes you slow the technique down in order to elicit the response you want from the opponent.

HONG TSEHAN IS FLANKED BY THOSE WHO HAVE HELPED BRING THIS ARTICLE TO FRUITION: ROBERT LIN-I YU (TRANSLATION) AND CHRIS BATES (TRANSLATION AND PHOTOGRAPHY).

## Techniques:
### Yanking Palm and Searching Palm

Two of the techniques in the first set of sequences—yanking palm (扽掌) and searching palm (探掌)—are typical. They start with the same technique used in many other sequences to establish contact with the opponent (1a–c), but diverge depending on opportunity. Simultaneous with a step to the outside angle facing your opponent, your leading hand wraps and pulls down on the opponent's opposite hand, a move that seems to "open the door" for him to strike (1b). If he strikes with the available hand, your next move blocks it with a piercing palm (穿掌) from the outside angle (1c).

The piercing palm converts to a grab while the leading hand now abandons its attachment to his opposite arm and flows up to launch a second piercing palm (1d). If he blocks with his free hand, grab that as well.

From this point there are other bifurcations in the attack that could lead to other sequences—for example, searching palm (1a–c+2d–e). You stand outside of the opponent, close the protective gate, transfer the first piercing-palm hand to the opponent's arm, and jerk his arm across his body, breaking his stability at the core. This is like pulling the wound-up string on a top. However, just at the moment when the opponent might start to adapt to the direction of the jerk, you change the course, yanking his momentum and body down, and then in the opposite direction (1d–e). The coup de grace of the sequence is a double palm strike cum push (1g–f).

Alternate follow-up.

76  Baguazhang • Hong Tsehan

# Wei Kuen Do

Adam James

**Where I Learned These Techniques**

The two techniques I've selected to discuss are the hook punch and the stepping cross punch, both superficially straightforward techniques, but each containing multitudes in terms of detail, refinement, and effectiveness. I learned these techniques from the founder and headmaster of the art of Wei Kuen Do, Grandmaster Leo Fong.

The hook punch is very effective against an aggressive opponent and allows the practitioner to move laterally during the exchange. It can be thrown while moving to the left or right, and comes straight at the opponent as the practitioner moves away. The result of combining hook punches with good footwork is that the punches come from all angles and the opponent doesn't know where the punches are coming from. During my years training with Leo, we worked on the subtle power of the hook and delivering it from a variety of angles. He taught me to take one technique and practice it until I could use it in a thousand ways, rather than practice a thousand techniques that can be used in only one way.

The stepping right cross is another very effective punch that can generate great power. To enhance positioning and change angles on the opponent, the right cross can also be thrown while stepping, but this type of punch can be very dangerous if it isn't practiced and performed with proper understanding of technique and positioning in the strike zone. I also learned this technique from Leo, who developed it from years of training in Western boxing and also from training with Bruce Lee and Angel Cabales, the founder of Serrada Escrima. Bruce Lee emphasized being relaxed and explosive with a whipping action. Angel Cabales used a V-step from Filipino martial arts to change angles and create power.

**Memorable Incidents Involving These Techniques**

I've used the hook punch in numerous situations. It can be very effective in combat sports, but also in self-defense. The left hook comes from a blind spot and it strikes a very vulnerable area. It can hit the temple, jawline, or behind the ear. It can also be targeted to the body and hit the ribs, kidney, or liver. I've used the stepping cross punch extensively over the last twenty years in my training with Leo Fong. The punch can be dangerous if a person doesn't understand proper technique and timing. However, once you perfect the punch, it allows you to change angles and generate tremendous power.

**Tips on Practicing the Techniques**

The left hook has remarkable power and often catches the opponent unawares because it comes from a blind spot. When practicing the hook punch, the practitioner must learn to use footwork and the jab to set it up. To throw an effective jab, one must be quick and explosive. Do not telegraph the movement. Immediately after the jab, slide to the side and throw the hook with a quick yet relaxed circular action. When delivering the left hook, it is greatly enhanced by leading with a jab and then hooking off the jab. The power in the hook punch comes from the whipping action and snap, not from throwing it with force. In fact, oftentimes, the harder a person throws the hook, the wider and wilder the punch becomes, making it telegraphic and ineffective. Conversely, the hook can be thrown with an open hand, like a slap, and this can be very effective in street fighting situations, providing a tremendous amount of force but not damaging the hand.

**The Stepping Cross Punch**

The stepping right cross is another very effective punch that can generate great power. To enhance the positioning and change angles on the opponent, however, the right cross can also be thrown while stepping. This type of punch can be very dangerous if it isn't practiced and performed with proper understanding of technique and positioning in the strike zone. The key for training with the stepping cross punch is to synchronize the step with the strike. From the fighting stance, step forward with the back foot while simultaneously striking with the right hand and sliding the front foot back. This punch can be executed with a variety of adjustments to the strike zone. One can step forward against a retreating opponent. Also, one can step and shift at the same distance in relationship to the strike zone and intercept the opponent with the stepping right cross. Lastly, one can make a quick, short step with the back foot while sliding the front foot back against the aggressive opponent who is moving straight forward.

For both of these techniques, as well as the rest of the Wei Kuen Do syllabus, the outward mechanics of the technique pale in comparison to the importance of generating internal energy, by virtue of having the appropriate mindset—developing a relaxed, explosive feeling and excellent timing.

## Technique 1: Left Hook (off the jab)

**1a)** James leads with a straight left jab, which the opponent parries with an open palm. **1b)** He moves with the inward/downward pressure of the block and uses it to circle down and around to the outside of the opponent's blocking arm. **1c)** As the jabbing hand escapes the parry, it remains loose and does not track too wide an arc (like a haymaker) while executing a hook punch. **1d)** James lands the hook punch on his opponent's jaw. **1e)** Reverse view, close-up of the impact point.

1a

1b

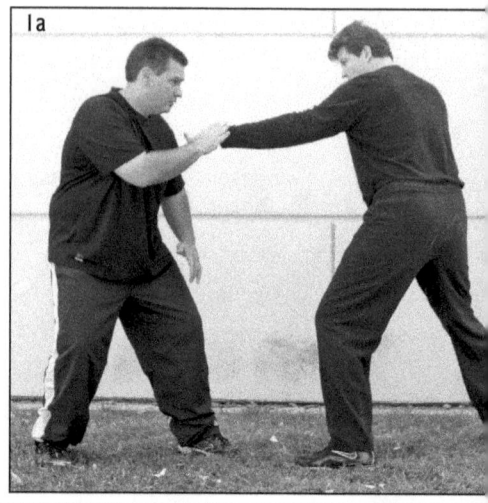

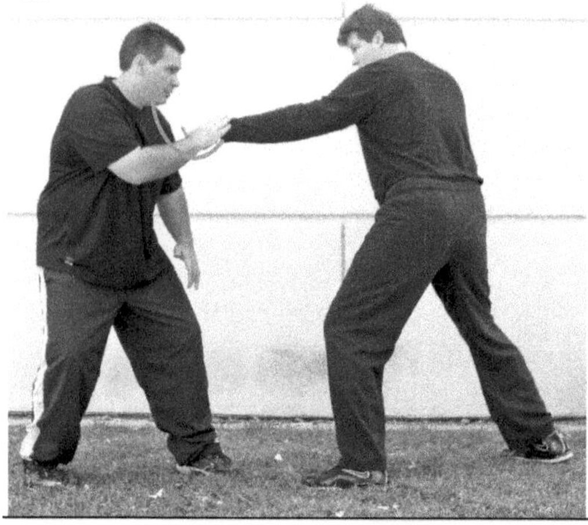

1c

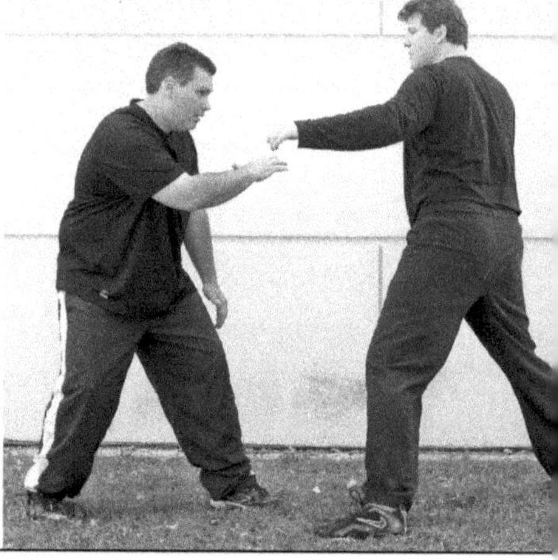

1d

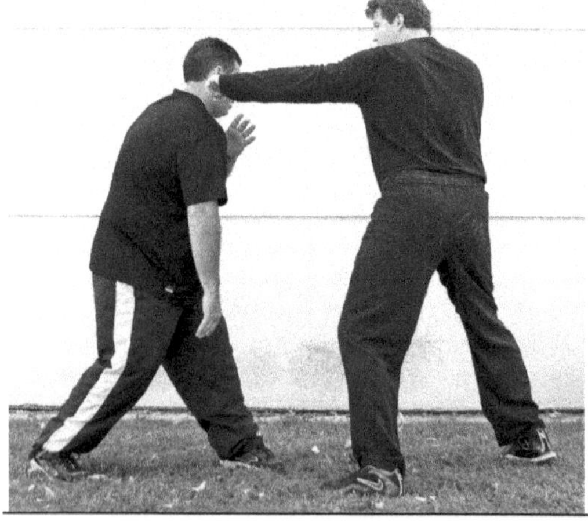

1e

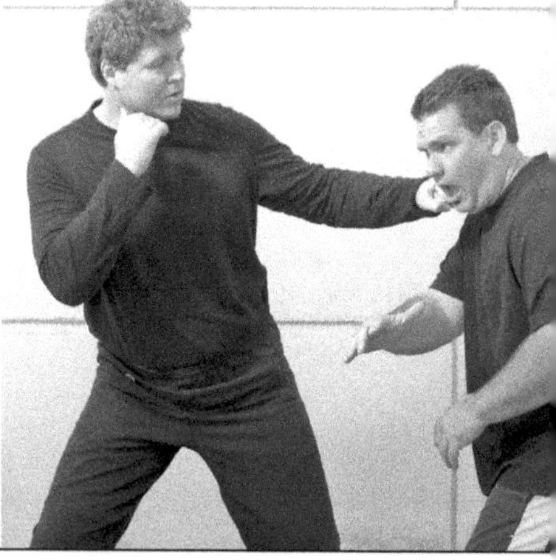

**Technique 2: The Stepping Cross Punch**

**2a)** James executes a right stepping cross punch with his right foot forward on impact; the key to this technique, however, is the footwork beforehand. **2b)** James begins in a fighting stance with his left foot forward. **2c)** He draws his right foot forward. **2d)** James continues to step forward with his right foot while simultaneously striking with his right hand and sliding the left foot back. **2e)** Completion of the footwork, and simultaneous delivery of the hand strike.

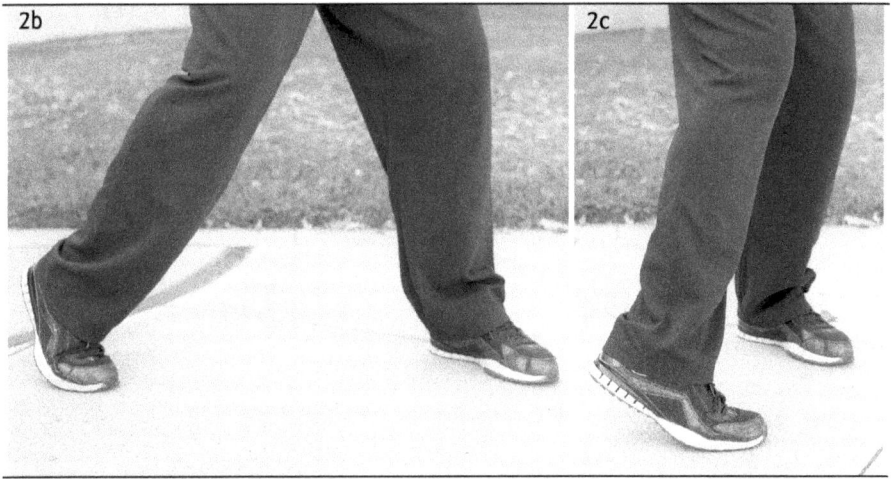

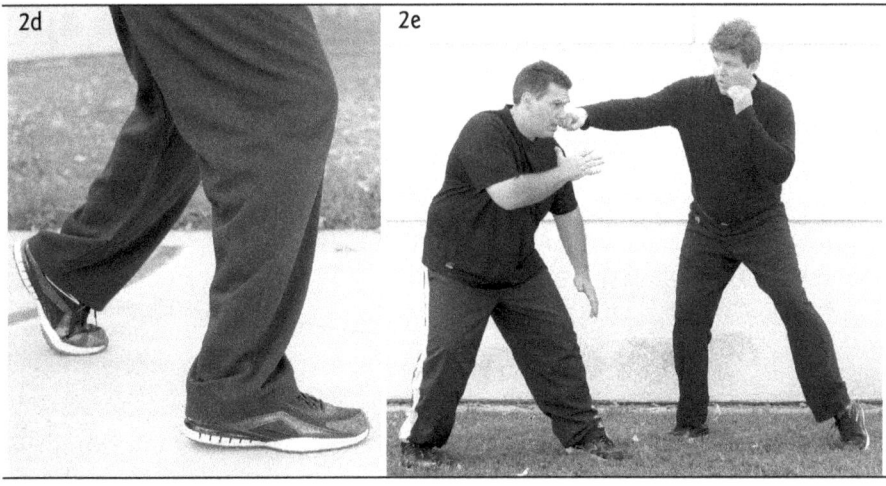

# Small Circle Jujitsu

Leon Jay

**Where I Learned These Techniques**

As the second generation headmaster of the art of Small Circle Jujitsu, I learned most of the techniques from my father, martial arts legend Wally Jay. My father was a student of Henry Okazaki, the headmaster of the Kodenkan style of jujutsu. In addition, Dad trained with such masters as Ken Kawachi (judo), Remy Presas (arnis), and Bruce Lee (Jeet Kune Do), each of whom he credits with having added to his martial arts expertise.

Much of the innovation of Small Circle Jujitsu is based on ideas that came to Wally Jay at unusual times and in unusual places. For example, his understanding of the art of palming came from practicing by pushing the three-wheeled carts he used when working as a mailman. And, as the second generation of this system, when new concepts came to my father overnight, I usually served as the training partner on whom these techniques were tested! The techniques selected for this article are two of my favorites.

**Memorable Incidents Involving These Techniques**

For self-defense, we should never miss an opportunity to throw a simple strike as a distracting or enabling technique during the execution of a lock or throw. While teaching what we call the "figure-four lock/throw" to a class one day, I noticed a pair of practitioners having some difficulty executing the technique smoothly. When I approached and asked what the problem was, they told me the thrower's elbow kept "accidentally" hitting the opponent's chin in the course of executing the technique!

It is sometimes said in the martial arts that for every attack, there is a defense—for every move, a counter. The Hawaiian choke might be the exception to the rule! Like the "naked hands interlock choke," the angle of the choker's forearms creates a triple threat for the unfortunate recipient, simultaneously restricting the airway, closing off the blood flow, and stimulating the vagus nerve. Unlike the "interlock choke," however, the off balancing and sideways positioning of the opponent preclude all readily available escape methods. The recipient is rendered helpless and also unconscious within a few seconds if the technique is applied with full force.

## Tips on Practicing the Techniques

The figure-four lock/throw technique is useful as a defense to a straight punch, which is easily slipped or deflected to the outside. The initial interception of the punch should be a deflection, not a hard blocking motion. Next the attacker's arm is grasped at the wrist, and the opponent is "softened up" with a strike to the head. Finally, the defender's striking arm creates the base over which the attacker's arm is folded to complete the technique.

Common defenses to the choke involve the recipient of the technique throwing the person applying the choke. These defenses all require the recipient to maintain his balance while causing the choker to lose his own. One of the primary advantages of the Hawaiian choke is that it takes the receiver completely off balance, preventing such defenses. This technique can be easily applied in response to a waist tackle, and begins as a simple reverse headlock. Rather than simply apply the choke from this static position, the defender uses the momentum of the tackle to continue to turn his opponent to the side. With the opponent completely off balance, the choke is then reinforced by clasping the palms together and applying a wringing action.

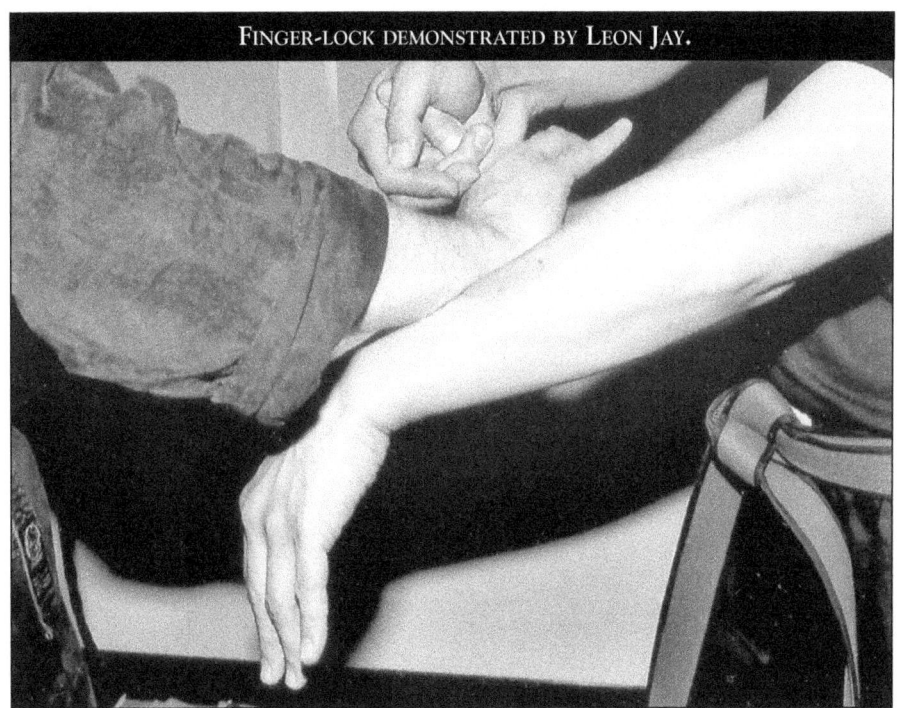
FINGER-LOCK DEMONSTRATED BY LEON JAY.

## Technique 1:
## Figure-Four Lock/Throw

**1a)** A straight punch is easily slipped or deflected to the outside. **1b)** The attacker's arm is grasped at the wrist. The opponent is "softened up" with a strike to the head. **1c)** The defender's arm creates the base over which the attacker's arm is folded. **1d)** Close-up of hand position for lock/throw. **1e)** Close-up of elbow strike while throwing.

## Technique 2:
## Hawaiian Choke

**2a)** The attacker attempts to tackle; the defender uses a reverse headlock.
**2b)** Close-up of reverse headlock.
**2c)** The defender uses the momentum to turn his opponent to the side.
**2d)** With the opponent off balance, the choke is then reinforced.
**2e)** Close-up of hand position on choke.

# Kodokan Judo

Llyr C. Jones, Ph.D.

This valedictory article is on Kodokan judo's *nage-no-kata* ("forms of throwing") and *katame-no-kata* ("forms of control"). Together, these katas form the *randori-no-kata* ("forms of free practice"), and their study helps facilitate the development of free practice (*randori*) skills.

During my formative years in judo, the emphasis in the United Kingdom was only on sports competitive judo, and kata practice had essentially been eliminated. There were no teachers with kata experience local to me, and so my early study of kata was self-directed through books. After developing competence in the mechanical movements of the randori-no-kata, I sought instruction from those judoka who had kept the kata flame alive in the UK, and over the years refined my skills under the guidance of some of the country's foremost kata experts, including Dai (David) Ball, the late Graham Wright, and Bob (Robert) Thomas. I would like to record my gratitude to those teachers now.

As an experienced judo player, I was privileged to develop further insight into katas through a memorable period of judo study in Japan. During my time spent at the Kodokan International Judo Institute in Tokyo and at various dojos in Kanagawa prefecture, I came to understand how the learning extractable from katas transcends that of merely developing physical skills and perfecting technique. While in Japan I cemented my belief that the link connecting judo's past, present, and future lies in the accurate teaching and practice of kata and it is this philosophy shapes my own kata practice, research, and teaching to this day.

Kata study is a challenging activity and achieving any degree of mastery will require many hours of patient and diligent study under the guidance of a knowledgeable teacher. However, as tips for their physical practice, the following elements should be considered essential. (In the following explanations, *tori* is the person who applies the technique, and *uke* is the person who receives the technique.)

- **Understanding:** An understanding of the fundamentals of the kata being demonstrated.
- **Logic:** Every movement in the kata must have a sensible purpose and be done in a sensible way. As such, one should always keep in mind the fundamental principles being demonstrated and the reason for the application of any particular technique.

- **Active Thought:** Katas should not be robotic, so one should actively think about one's role (as either tori or uke) and whether one is initiating or responding, attacking or defending, escaping or adjusting, etc.
- **Composure:** Proper concentration, decorum, and attitude.
- **Commitment:** Real attacks and real defenses.
- **Tempo:** Each kata has its own speed and tempo. Within some (e.g., the nage-no-kata) the tempo also varies from move to move, while others have one tempo.
- **Fluidity:** The kata must "flow" since any performance will break down if there is hesitation during application.
- **Posture:** Balance and body control.
- **Coordination:** Between tori and uke in the techniques themselves, but also in the movements and transition between techniques.
- **Positioning:** Awareness of one's location on the mat with proper engagement distance, direction, and spacing.
- *Reigei:* Correct etiquette.

Kata practice should go beyond merely performing physical movements, and during practice one should always think about how kata can improve one's judo in the broader sense. The following are tips on assimilating and leveraging the lessons of randori-no-kata into everyday judo.

▶ **Nage-no-Kata:** Consisting of five sets of three throws, each performed to the left and right sides, this kata helps develop an understanding of the theoretical basis of judo and the processes involved in *kuzushi*, *tsukuri*, and *kake*—i.e., how to assume the correct position for applying a throwing technique once uke's balance has been broken, and how to apply and complete a technique. This kata has uke attacking tori fifteen times—each time learning and adjusting his attack based on tori's previous response. Tori neutralizes uke's attack each time by applying himself and using the force or action of the attack itself to prevail. Tori also learns how his own body and mind react under physical and psychological stress, and also how to adapt effectively to changing circumstances utilizing both his body and mind.

▶ **Katame-no-Kata:** Consisting of three sets of five grappling techniques, this kata helps develop an understanding of the theoretical basis for learning control through executing and evading each technique. Tori learns how to best use his body in an efficient manner to control uke on the ground through working on his versatility and body movement while grappling. Similarly, uke, through striving to escape, learns how to exploit any weaknesses in tori's technique. Each and every time the katame-no-kata is practiced, uke should continue to test tori by looking for his weak points and then attacking them, while tori should find new ways of nullifying uke's new escape attempts.

## Sequence 1

1a) Shoulder wheel (*kata-guruma*) from the first set—hand techniques (*te waza*).
1b) Lift-pull hip throw (*tsurikomi-goshi*) from the second set—hip techniques (*koshi waza*).
1c) Inner-thigh throw (*uchi mata*) from the third set—leg techniques (*ashi waza*).
1d) Rear throw (*ura nage*) from the fourth set—supine sacrifice techniques (*ma sutemi waza*).
1e) Side hook (*yoko-gake*) from the fifth set—side sacrifice techniques (*yoko sutemi waza*).

## Sequence 2

2a) Broken top four-corner hold (*kuzure kami shiho-gatame*) from the first set—holding techniques (*osae-komi waza*).
2b) Naked lock (*hadaka-jime*) from the second set—strangling techniques (*shime waza*).
2c) Arm crush (*ude gatame*) from the third set—joint techniques (*kansetsu waza*).

*All photographs copyright Carl De Crée (2007) and used with permission.*

⬅ From a nage-no-kata performance at the First Kodokan Judo Kata International Tournament, 2007.
Tori: Katsuyuki Kondo, sixth dan.
Uke: Tetsushi Okouchi, fifth dan.

⬇ From a katame-no-kata performance at the First Kodokan Judo Kata International Tournament, 2007.
Tori: Kazutaka Yamamoto, seventh dan.
Uke: Hirao Nasu, sixth dan.

# Muso Shinden-ryu Iaido

Deborah Klens-Bigman, Ph.D.

### Drawing, Cutting, and Resheathing the Japanese Sword

All styles of Japanese swordsmanship have two common characteristics: the draw, which frequently includes a cut (*nukitsuke*), and resheathing (*noto*). The draw-cut and resheathing are very basic techniques, yet even advanced students struggle to master them. My teacher, Otani Yoshiteru, often remarked that if the draw-cut was no good, the rest of the form did not matter. Japanese sword forms are based on hypothetical attack and defense situations; therefore, good drawing and cutting technique is fundamental to the "success" of the practitioner's effort against an attacker. Resheathing may be less important as a tactic, but proper technique (along with *chiburi*, shaking blood off of the sword) identifies the practitioner as a member of a specific style, and, more important, allows the sword to be resheathed safely. I will briefly note important points for proper drawing, cutting, and resheathing based on my twenty-six-year study of Muso Shinden-ryu (夢想神伝流) iaido; however, these points can be adapted to other styles of Japanese swordsmanship as well.

When I began practicing Japanese swordsmanship, Otani was frequently absent on business, so the upperclassmen made sure we got our fill of basics. At my second practice, one of them tried to instill the importance of a proper draw-cut, having me rise from a kneeling posture over and over, drawing and attempting to cut. No one told me I should have purchased knee pads for working on the very inhospitable floor. Over and over again, I rose to my knees, stepped out with my right foot, and drew the sword, a clunky, chipped loaner from the group. For the better part of an hour, the upperclassman insisted that I had to "see" my enemy in order to make an effective cut. Finally, knees aching and shoulders weary, I visualized him as my target, and made my best cut yet.

"Yes! That's what I'm talking about," he exclaimed.

Damn right, I thought.

We practiced drawing, cutting, and resheathing through long sessions of *batto-noto*—drawing with a cut; performing a short, sharp blood-flicking movement (*kochiburi*); and resheathing—on our knees. I eventually did it properly after many hours of practice.

A proper draw-cut begins with the sword grip situated at the center of the body. The draw must be silent. Any noise means the sheath is being damaged by the sword, which can cut through or split the sheath, causing potentially serious injury. The sword is drawn toward the opponent at the same time the sheath is drawn back (*sayabiki*). The right hand grip is very relaxed to begin with, and the cut itself begins just as the sword tip leaves the sheath by tightening the fingers, starting with the little finger and working across to the index finger. The resulting cut should snap out in a controlled manner, ending at the proper place (in the Muso Shinden beginning form Shohatto, the cut ends just across the opponent's face).

*iaido*

Proper resheathing cannot be overemphasized, as serious injury can result from improper technique. I once attended a seminar where the teacher emphasized cutting targets over any other technique. During the demonstration offered at the end of practice, his students cut well, but I was horrified at his chief student's uncertainty and lack of technique in returning the razor-sharp sword to the sheath. I wanted to leave the room, but made myself stay, thinking I might have to perform first aid to keep someone from bleeding to death! Needless to say, I lost respect for the seminar teacher in a heartbeat.

We learned proper resheathing primarily by practicing the batto-noto exercise noted above. From time to time an upperclassman would stand behind a newcomer, physically pulling the sheath for *sayabiki*, a technique I still use for my students.

Good resheathing technique depends on the grip of the left hand on the sheath, and pulling back the sheath. The student places the thumb at the tips of the middle and index fingers, which cover the mouth of the sheath (*koiguchi*). The student's fingers, once positioned, must never move until the end of the resheathing, when only the metal collar at the base of the blade is exposed. For resheathing in Muso Shinden-ryu's beginning set of forms, the blade is placed across the fingers of the left hand, starting at the base of the blade. The practitioner draws the blade to the right as the left hand pulls the sheath around to the back. The tip of the sword drops into the sheath. The sheath moves to meet the blade—the blade does not swing around to the mouth of the sheath. At the end of the resheathing, the grip of the sword should once again be in the center of the body, as it was at the start of the draw.

**Technique I**

1a) Hand position for beginning draw with a cut (note soft grip of the right hand).
1b) Full extension of draw before the start of the cut.
1c) Full draw with a cut (for the form Shohatto).
1d) Full draw from the rear, showing the sheath partially pulled back.

*Photography by Takashi Ikezawa.*

## Technique 2

**2a)** Left hand position for the start of resheathing. **2b)** Starting position for resheathing as it is done in the beginning set of forms, at the base of the blade.
**2c)** Pulling the sword tip across the left hand, just prior to its insertion in the sheath.
**2d)** The sheath fully pulled around during resheathing, shown from the rear.

# Sambo

Stephen Koepfer, M.A., L.M.T.

**Where I Learned This Technique**

I have had a love for the scarf hold almost since my first days training grappling. It is an incredibly practical and versatile top control position that is commonly overlooked in the submission-grappling world.

It is hard to know exactly where I learned the scarf hold I teach today. Certainly, my primary Sambo coach, Alexander Barakov, first introduced me to the finer details of the position when I started training with him in 1999. However, since that time I have had the pleasure of learning from many notable coaches, including Igor Kurinnoy, Oleg Taktarov, and Igor Yakimov. Likewise, I have been lucky enough to train alongside such Sambists as Gregg Humphreys, Aaron Fields, Doug Fournet, and Dayn DeRose. All these men and others have contributed to my knowledge base. So, it is really by standing on the shoulders of my peers that my knowledge of the scarf hold evolved to what I teach today.

**Memorable Incidents Involving This Technique**

The scarf hold came to my attention when I first dipped my toes in the pool of the competition world outside of sport karate and other point-sparring events during the early 1990s. Then, in 1997, I entered my first MMA-style fight, a Shooto-rules fight. I had not yet started training Sambo and was relying on my Taekwondo and Sanshou background, as well as some rudimentary grappling I had learned.

The fight started out well enough. My stand-up game was decent and I landed a few shots. But, I was facing a wrestler. When the inevitable happened and he took me down to the mat, I was doomed. He put me in a scarf hold and proceeded to smother me like a python until I could no longer breathe. The fight was over. I lost. Yet, it was at that moment that I knew I loved the scarf hold.

As a coach, the scarf hold has become a staple position I use and I teach to all my students. Over and over again I see my students use the scarf hold to gain critical advantage over their opponents, be it to score a pin, gain control before moving on to a submission, or simply secure an opponent in order to deliver some strikes. Without question, the scarf hold is a position that allows one to impose his will. It is not uncommon for opponents to approach us after matches to comment on how difficult the position is to overcome.

**Tips on Practicing This Technique**

When applying the scarf hold, there are a few principles that must be followed. First is to relax into the hold. The more relaxed you are, the heavier you are. Your body weight used in tandem with gravity and technique makes this position powerful. The tenser you are, the less mobile you will be, and the easier you will be to counter. Second, keep your position high on your opponent's chest, keep your legs away from his legs, and keep your hips and center of gravity as low as possible. This will help compress your opponent's chest, making it much more difficult for him to breathe. It will keep your legs out of range of your opponent's legs for a counter. Finally, keep your opponent's head off the mat and follow his breath. Keeping your opponent's head raised will significantly decrease his ability to bridge and escape your scarf hold. It will also bring his mouth and nose toward your chest to restrict breathing. As you settle into the position, follow your opponent's breath. With each exhalation he makes, settle in deeper and constrict a bit tighter. Breath is life, and if you take that from your opponent, he has little chance to defeat you.

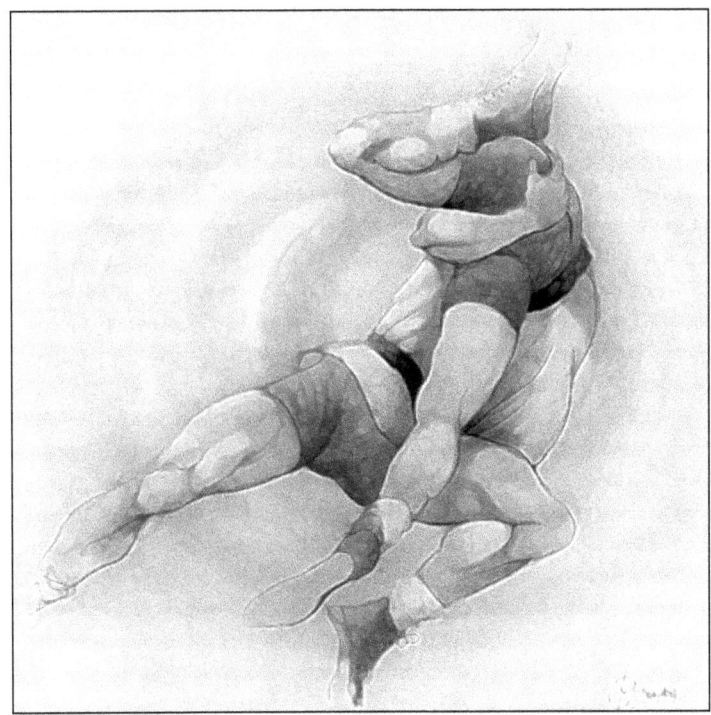

**Sambo in action.**

*Illustration by Oscar Ratti.*

## Technique 1: Transition to Shoulder Lock from Scarf Hold

1a) Stephen secures this hold by keeping low, holding his opponent's head off the mat, and keeping his legs out of range. 1b) Hooking his opponent's arm and keeping his body weight pressed onto his opponent, Stephen transitions to an arm attack. 1c) Keeping close contact, Stephen kneels on the far side of his opponent's head and places his shin against his back. This offers strong neck and back control of the opponent. 1d) While kneeling over his opponent, Stephen secures a tight figure-four grip on the target arm with the opponent's triceps secured against his chest. He keeps his opponent's hand away from his jacket which he could grab hold of to defend the submission. 1e) Stephen rotates his opponent's arm toward the rear for a shoulder lock.

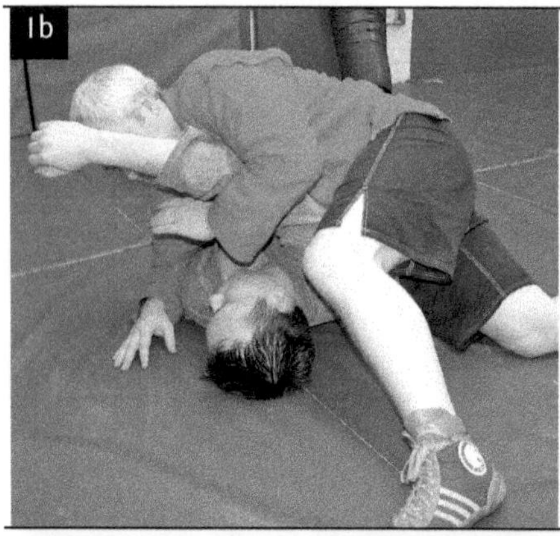

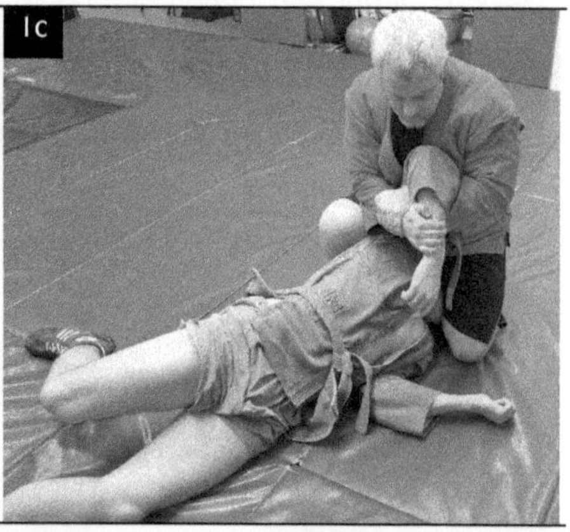

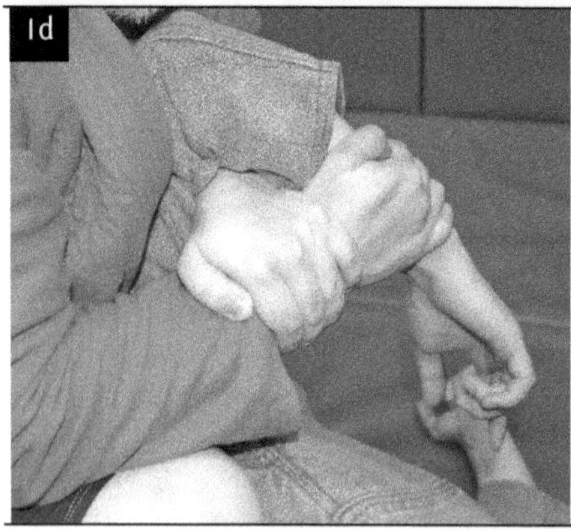

## Technique 2: Kneebar Counter to Failed Scarf Hold

**2a)** Stephen secures his hold by keeping his opponent's head off the mat and legs out of range. **2b)** Stephen's opponent manages to begin a counter. He hooks Stephen's leg in an attempt to take Stephen's back. **2c)** As a re-counter, Stephen hooks his opponent's bottom leg with his foot. **2d)** As the opponent attempts to take his back, Stephen abandons the scarf hold. Using his re-counter hook, Stephen pulls his opponent's leg toward his own chest. **2e)** To finish the kneebar, Stephen hugs the target leg close to his chest, locks his opponent's instep on his shoulder, secures leg control by tightly pinching his knees together, places his heels on his opponent's butt for leverage, and slowly bridges forward to hyperextend the knee.

# Goju-ryu Karate

Marvin Labbate

This article presents Okinawan Goju-ryu karate-do as a kata-based training system. It brings together kata-based training elements for various levels of understanding and application, combining solo principles and partner-based training principles. At its most basic level, a kata is a form or pattern of movements that train various fighting scenarios and responses. At the most advanced level, for which katas serve as the encyclopedia of the entire martial art, katas provide a sequence of dangerous to deadly techniques. Between the two extremes are levels of development to which masters have historically controlled access. While these restrictions were to ensure that only those with appropriate moral, spiritual, and physical preparation were able to use and teach these ideas, in modern times these restrictions have been relaxed for commercial gain. Thus, it is more important than ever to address responsible training and use of these principles.

As this article will discuss, the art of Goju-ryu is also a system. While karate training can be "performance based" for showy applications such as tournaments, traditional training for self-defense is kata based, and thus the center of the Goju-ryu system is also kata-based training. Each series of kata movements has a translation—the basic form and pattern—but it has many applications. Thus, while "practicing" a kata provides a first step, if the karate practitioner wishes to fully grasp a kata's richness, he or she will explore these applications. Furthermore, while the understandings and applications of the kata will vary, the basic system applies to any and all katas. As I will describe below, this system includes familiarizing oneself with the background of the kata, working through solo and partner training, and developing a self-defense repertoire based on traditional kumite sets.

It is helpful to approach any kata by familiarizing oneself with some historical and technical background. One combines a general awareness of karate-related culture, philosophy, etiquette, and language with kata-specific information, such as the name of the kata, its definition or meaning, and its history or origins (such as why and how it was developed, when, where, and with whom). By studying the background of a kata, the karate practitioner gains insight that can help develop the kata and its applications. He understands that historically there have been various levels of kata application: obvious techniques; intermediate-level applications that must be taught; individual interpretations through which the black belt ranks are able to become artists; and *okuden*, or hidden techniques and principles that historically masters did not transmit except to select individuals with sufficient merit. Through this background, a kata is understood as a deep, meaningful source of martial knowledge. Then the practitioner moves on to training in the kata itself.

Kata-based training has two major components: solo and partner training. In solo training, one begins with memorizing the pattern of a kata, its basic steps and movements. Once the pattern is mastered, principles are layered over and integrated with the movements. Among others, key principles include the sanchin kata's principles of structure, movement, and breathing, and karate drum principles of generating close-range power. Thus, the elementary movements of the kata are broken into parts that are drilled in order to internalize the basics and develop the specific kata. This layered solo training gives basic body mechanics and allows the kata to evolve. Solo movement is then further developed by moving with a partner. Partner training adds elements such as distancing, timing of entering and exiting, and awareness. This phase includes practices such as *tai sabaki* (body shifting, or giving up space without giving up ground) and *kakie* (push-hands, or sensitivity training, which teaches how the partner will move without having to watch).

In order to practice and develop kata-based training (whether novice, intermediate, or advanced) into a fighting or self-defense repertoire of techniques, one then follows a formula based on traditional sparring sets, some of which are presented here in the diagrams below. These kumite sets can include the following: basic *bunkai*, or one-step attacks with defense and counter taken from kata sequences; advanced bunkai that combine the basic moves with takedowns; flow drills that teach how to flow from one move to another with a partner; basic grappling; advanced grappling with the application of choking techniques; two-person katas; freestyle drills; and other variations. Together, these elements develop any kata at any level as an effective means of self-defense.

The steps for the kata-based training system are the same for any kata. A single step, sweep, and shuto technique—from a novice Goju-ryu kata called Gekisai-Dai-Ichi—is presented here in order to illustrate the fact that when combining the principles and formula, the basics are the best techniques. By following the system, one can defend oneself even with a basic kata. As part of individual karate practice, however, the practitioner will apply the training system to different katas based on his or her individual body, skills, and gifts.

## Basic Tegumi (Grappling) Kumite

1a) The attacker and defender are in traditional grappling stances.

1b) The defender throws a right slap to the left side of the attacker's neck.

1c) The defender follows through with his right hand and sweeps the attacker's front leg.

1d) The defender throws a right shuto to the right side of the attacker's neck.

1e) The defender's arm continues around the attacker's neck, forcing him down.

1f) The defender applies a choke.

## Jiyu Kumite (Freestyle Sparring)

2a) The attacker and defender pair off in sparring stances.

2b) The defender grabs the attacker's leading hand and chambers.

*Acknowledgments to Greg Macedin and John Nelson for help with the demonstrations; Jill Petersen Adams, assistant; and Scott Gardner, photography.*

2c) The defender steps in and sweeps the attacker's leading leg.

2d) The defender throws a shuto across the attacker's neck.

# Mixed Martial Arts

Tim Lajcik, B.A.

### Where I Learned These Techniques

What's known as "mixed martial arts" (MMA) is not an organized system of self-defense, rather it is a sport that draws from many martial arts and combative disciplines. I have selected two effective MMA counter techniques that also have practical application in self-defense situations. The first, the double-wristlock counter versus a single-leg takedown attack, is a variation of judo's reverse *ude-garami*, or what is often referred to as a "kimura" in Brazilian Jiujitsu (named in deference to the great judo player Kimura Masahiko, who used the reverse ude-garami to defeat and break the arm of Brazilian Jiujitsu cofounder Helio Gracie). The second technique is a parry and straight right counter versus a left jab, a boxing tactic which borrows from principles of gongfu parries.

I was taught this variation of the double wristlock by a former training partner, Eric Duus, a wrestler and judo player who was nationally ranked in both sports. Duus wrestled at the University of Wisconsin, where he was coached by and learned the technique from world and Olympic champion Dave Shultz, a brilliant wrestling technician.

I learned the parry and straight right counter from Eugene Ray, my first boxing coach, a former California state kickboxing champion and trainer of world champion kickboxer Dennis Alexio.

### Memorable Incidents Involving These Techniques

The aforementioned Dave Schultz's younger brother and protégé, Mark Schultz, also a world and Olympic champion, used the double-wristlock counter to great effect in the 1984 Olympic Games, breaking the elbow of the defending world champion from Turkey. Mark was subsequently disqualified from the match when the hold was deemed illegal. However, with the Turk unable to continue, Mark went on to dominate the remainder of his bouts and capture the gold medal. Notably, the Olympic wrestling governing body took the unprecedented measure of assigning an additional referee to scrutinize the Schultz brothers' remaining Olympic matches for unduly dangerous techniques. Dave, incidentally, also emerged from the same Olympic Games with a gold medal.

The parry and right-hand counter holds personal significance because I used it to score a knockout in my first amateur boxing bout as well as a Sanshou championship fight. Sentimentality aside, besides being a potent "fight ender," this technique has, over the years, proven extremely useful in dismantling my opponents' striking offense. That is, by giving my opponent a negative consequence for throwing his left jab, he becomes less likely to throw subsequent jabs. This has a ripple effect, for if my opponent does not establish his jab, he will be hard-pressed to set up his straight right punch. And, finally, without a straight right, he loses a reliable means for setting up his left hook.

**Tips on Practicing These Techniques**

As with any technique that carries a high potential for injuring your opponent, it's important to execute the double-wristlock counter in a controlled manner when drilling or sparring. In practice, your initial focus will be on developing the neuromuscular patterning to efficiently secure your opponent's wrist with the proper double-wristlock grip. With your training partner seizing your leg, execute this grip again and again, progressively increasing the speed until you are able to secure it seamlessly and without thinking of the configuration of your hands and arms. Next, practice "popping" your hip against your partner's shoulder to break his grip on your leg and to isolate the arm you have secured. Have your partner secure progressively a tighter grip, which will require increasingly explosive action in the hips to break. Finally, become familiar with the path in which you will move your partner's secured arm away from his body for maximum effect. Progress through this movement very slowly (taking ten seconds or more) until your partner signals verbally and with a hard tap of his free hand on your thigh that he feels the potential for damage to his elbow, his shoulder, or both. Release your hold instantly upon your partner's signal.

When executing the parry and straight right counter, be mindful not to extend your arm or square your hips and shoulder to meet your opponent's jab. Doing this will exhaust the potential energy for your punch before it has been thrown. Practice patience. Allow his jab to come to you. Catch and parry the jab two or three inches in front of your face. Let that contact be the trigger for your hip and shoulder to initiate your counterpunch. Once you have a grasp of the technique's mechanics against your partner's jab, have him periodically feint his jab. If his feint is well-executed, you will likely "bite" on the feint. However, if the action for your parry is in the wrist rather than the elbow, as it should be, you will not find your arm extended and face exposed for the real jab that follows the feint.

## Double-Wristlock Counter versus Single-Leg Attack

1a) Transfer your weight to the leg that your opponent is attempting to secure. 1b) Seize your opponent's wrist first, as illustrated; then thread your opposite hand over your opponent's arm and grab your own wrist.
1c) Close-up of the double-wristlock hold. 1d) Pop your hips to break your opponent's grip on your leg.
1e) Rotate your opponent's arm toward the line of his spine and away from his back for the submission.

*Partner: Brhett Butler. Photographer: Alexey Koleskinov.*

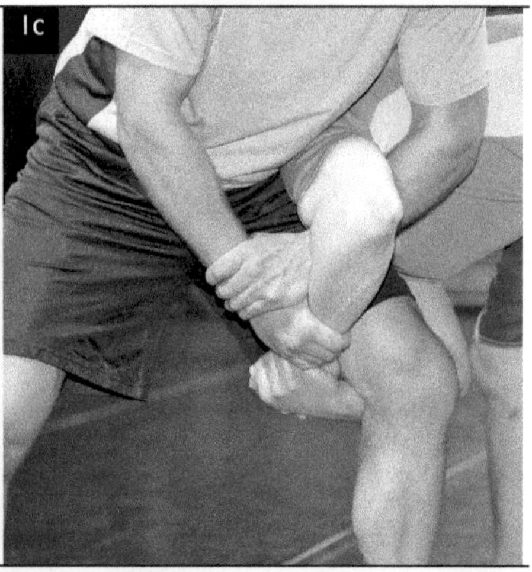

## Parry and Straight Right Counter versus Left Jab

**2a)** Face your opponent, both in a conventional boxing stance. **2b)** Catch your opponent's left jab close to your face with the heel of your cupped right hand. **2c)** Turn your wrist so the thumb side of your hand moves down and away, slightly deflecting your opponent's left jab. **2d)** As your fingers "climb" over your opponent's deflected jab, make your own fist. **2e)** Execute a straight right punch to your opponent's jaw.

Asian Martial Arts • Practical Applications

# Zheng-Style Taijiquan

Russ Mason, M.A.

### Practical Applications of Taiji's Ward-off and Diagonal Flying Postures

Ward-off is one of the fundamental postures of Yang-style Taijiquan. The Chinese character for ward-off is *peng* (掤), an obscure pictogram containing elements representing "hand" and "twin moons" reflecting each other as "friends." Another theory posits that the origin of *peng* may be a primitive character for the tail of the legendary phoenix, a bird symbolic of natural harmony and yin-yang balance. Both images present a good metaphor for the principles of sticking and following, which are essential to the application of Taiji boxing. As a signature technique of the art, ward-off employs *peng jin* (掤勁), an outwardly expanding energy that is further developed in the diagonal flying posture. Applications of the ward-off left and diagonal flying postures will be illustrated here.

Zheng Manqing was a disciple of Yang Chengfu and the creator of the thirty-seven-posture Yang short form, which he taught to my instructors who, in turn, passed the art to me. Zheng taught that the ultimate principle of Taijiquan resides in the application of neutralization and the substance of central equilibrium (*zhong ding*). Attacking energy is received and, through yielding and neutralizing, redirected around one's constant central axis. Therefore, the principles of neutralization, sticking, and following permeate every application of Taijiquan. Accordingly, the ward-off posture is primarily soft, receptive, and perceptive (like a cricket's antenna); however, ward-off energy (an expanding energy that rises upward and outward) can be used to issue energy as well as to sense it.

While learning the solo form as a beginning Taijiquan student, my first encounter with ward-off left me puzzled. Since I had heard that Taijiquan eschews blocking, the use of this posture seemed mysterious until I experienced its application at the hands of Zheng Manqing's senior student, Benjamin Pang Jeng Lo. At a workshop hosted by Robert W. Smith in the 1970s, I had a chance to cross arms with Mr. Lo. As soon as he touched me, to my astonishment, I felt completely vulnerable, as if through that contact he could perceive my intentions. His eyes dancing with amusement, Mr. Lo used his soft ward-off arm to totally control me, literally wiping the floor with my sprawling body. Two decades later, my understanding of the function deepened as Liu Xiheng, head of Zheng's Taipei school, used his profoundly relaxed ward-off arm and an almost imperceptible whole-body movement to effortlessly receive my attack and send me flying several meters away.

In applying ward-off, one must remain soft, alert, and sensitive. The body is relaxed, rooted, and balanced, always maintaining central equilibrium. First, one must receive and yield to the opponent's attack, perceiving its force and direction and following the attacker's intention. After the attack has been neutralized and controlled, the attacker's body will be disordered and unbalanced, leaving an opportunity for counterattack. One must be careful not to resist force with force. By joining with rather than blocking the attacking limb, the energy of the attack can be stored and returned.

The diagonal flying posture appears in only a right-handed version in Professor Zheng's system. It consists of a more complex series of transitional movements culminating in a flamboyant extended attack that extrapolates the ideas introduced by ward-off. I vividly remember the moment of stunned terror I felt when Robert W. Smith applied this technique with a lightning fast thrust to my throat, gripping my trachea expertly and inextricably between his thumb and index finger. His firm but gentle grasp did not injure me, but left no doubt in my mind of the potential lethality of the technique.

The diagonal flying posture includes a deep, 135-degree step and turn, suggesting a wide range of movement, and the hands move through splitting, tearing, and piercing actions. Finally, the articulation of the right arm and the waist suggests a "folding" technique in which the downward energy of an arm grab above the elbow is converted circularly to a thrusting attack by folding the elbow down and extending the hand forward.

The final piercing extension of the upturned palm in diagonal flying can be used to attack the throat by spearing, grasping, or striking. The "V" created by the right thumb and index finger of the upturned right hand can grasp the cricoid cartilage surrounding the opponent's larynx and thyroid, or slightly below that, where the trachea meets the larynx. The first joint of the index finger can apply pressure to the common carotid artery as the thumb presses into the windpipe or internal jugular vein. Alternatively, the posture may be used to lock the opponent's right arm or, with an outward rotation of the palm, forearm, and waist, the technique can be modified to create an unbalancing deflection or a throw using the knife edge of the downturned hand against the side of the neck.

Like ward-off, diagonal flying can be an effective counter to a right or left punch, or a front kick. The essence of the application is in yielding and following, so the exact articulation of the counterattack depends on the situation and the opponent's responses.

## Technique 1: Ward-off

1a) Russ Mason neutralizes Erik Flannigan's left punch, controlling the arm with ward-off's transitional "hold the ball" stance. 1b) After blending with and sticking to the attack, Mason shifts and follows Flannigan's retreat, stepping in and controlling his balance with ward-off. 1c) Mason sits deeply into ward-off to uproot and discharge Flannigan. 1d) Alternatively, Mason neutralizes Flannigan's right punch. 1e) Mason unbalances Flannigan and shifts weight to the right foot while pivoting left, throwing him.

### Technique 2: Diagonal Flying

**2a)** Mason neutralizes Flannigan's right front kick, capturing the leg. **2b)** He uses diagonal flying to attack Flannigan's throat, immobilizing his right leg and controlling his balance. **2c)** Mason uses a throat attack to unbalance and throw Flannigan. **2d)** Alternatively, Mason uses diagonal flying against his right punch to lock Flannigan's arm and break his root. **2e)** Mason uses a knife-edge hand and whole-body power against Flannigan's neck to unbalance and throw him.

Thanks to colleague Erik Flannigan (3rd dan TKD) for assistance with the demonstrations and to Laurie Fuhrmann for the photography.

# Ryukyu Kobudo Shinkokai

Mario McKenna, M.Sc.

## Where I Learned These Techniques

Most karate practitioners are familiar with the tonfa, bo, sai, and nunchaku as they are practiced in many karatedo dojos around the world, but Ryukyu Kobudo, the weapons tradition of Okinawa, encompasses a wider range of weaponry than just these four. This was the extent of my knowledge until I moved to Japan and began studying Ryukyu Kobudo formally with Minowa Katsuhiko and Yoshimura Hiroshi. Under their tutelage I learned that Ryukyu Kobudo uses a plethora of different weapons that are supported by multiple katas and two-person sets. One of those weapons I was introduced to is the *tekko*, or *tikko*, as Minowa preferred to call it.

It was during my second year of practice that I first encountered the tekko, and my initial thought was that it resembles a "knuckle duster." After being handed a pair, it was obvious that this weapon was much "meatier" than a "knuckle duster"; it was thicker, denser, and heavier—it clearly had intent. Yoshimura told me the tekko was a *kakushi buki*, or concealed weapon, that was popular for self-defense in old Okinawa, since it is relatively small and easy to conceal.

For several months I was drilled in *Maezato no tekko*, the kata that supports the techniques for the tekko. This kata is named after its creator, Minowa sensei's teacher, Shinken Taira (1897–1970). Once I had gained some proficiency with the tekko, I was slowly introduced to the two-person fighting set.

## Memorable Incidents Involving These Techniques

I had been practicing both the kata and two-person set for a year and was starting to feel more comfortable with them. Along the way there were the usual mishaps, mostly self-inflicted, but not always. Yoshimura sensed my surge in confidence and, like any good teacher, decided to push the boundaries a little. The next time we practiced the two-person fighting set, he went a little harder and a little faster. Tekko in hand, I was the defender, but I struggled to keep up and it was obvious my technique wasn't good enough yet. Minowa looked over and said, "*Mada desu*"; you don't have it right yet.

A few months later I was facing Yoshimura again, but this time I was the attacker. Bo in hand, I delivered the strikes with all the vigor and stupidity of youth. A few sequences into the set, I felt a sharp pain on my fingers and dropped the bo to the floor. Yoshimura had given me a light tap with the tekko. Nothing was broken, no blood, but that light tap taught me how dangerous and debilitating this weapon can be in the proper hands. It is a lesson I never forgot.

**Tips on Practicing These Techniques**

Although the original two-person set has the attacker using a bo, the techniques are not limited to countering only that weapon. They can be applied equally against empty-hand attacks or bladed weapons. To that end, it is important to become accustomed to different combative engagement distances and their associated timing (*maai*). When practicing these techniques, I recommend progressing through different ranges and weapons until proficiency is reached:

1. close range (e.g., empty hand)
2. short range (e.g., knife or stick)
3. midrange (e.g., four-foot staff), and
4. long range (e.g., six-foot staff)

When using the tekko as a weapon of self-defense, there are two key points you should bear in mind. The first is to not become trapped in a block-and-counter paradigm. This is not only slow and unrealistic, but also potentially dangerous to the defender. Instead, attack and defense are to be used simultaneously. That is, the tekko must be used to strike vulnerable parts of the opponent's body as he attacks. Strikes should be aimed at the joints of the body, as this inhibits or stops the attacker from using his own weapons. The second point is that footwork (*taisabaki*) is extremely important for fist-loaded weapons like the tekko. You must not only avoid the attack, but place yourself in an advantageous position to deliver your own. The following photographs illustrate the use of the tekko against the empty hand.

**Acknowledgements**

I would like to extend my sincerest thanks to Maik Hassel for the fine photography work, and Brent Zarparniuk for posing as the *kosha* (opponent) in the photographs.

## Technique 1:
### Overhead Deflection and Low Strike

1a) Face your opponent with your left foot forward in a natural stance. Both hands are in front of your torso with the left hand leading. 1b) As the opponent moves forward to punch, step forward with the right foot, and raise both hands to catch the opponent's arm at the elbow. *Key point*: Take a deep step forward into the opponent;

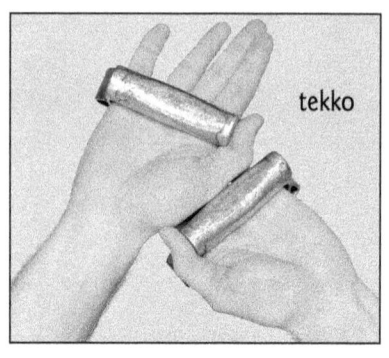
tekko

palms are open when performing the over-head deflection with the right hand on top of the left hand (see tekko detail). 1c) Shift your weight onto your lead leg and press up with both palms to unbalance the opponent. *Key point*: To clear the attack, spring the hands up and away. 1d) Shift your weight onto your right leg, bend your torso, and strike down in front of you with both hands on the opponent's knee. *Key point*: Use the handles of the tekko to strike the opponent. The thumbs apply pressure to the top of the tekko for stability.

## Technique 2:
## Midlevel Counterstrike

**2a)** Face your opponent with your left foot forward in a natural stance. Both hands are in front of your torso with the left hand leading. **2b)** Pivot to the right, step in with your right foot and deliver a left vertical punch. *Key points*: *Shift your weight to your rear leg as you pivot; stabilize the tekko by pressing down with* 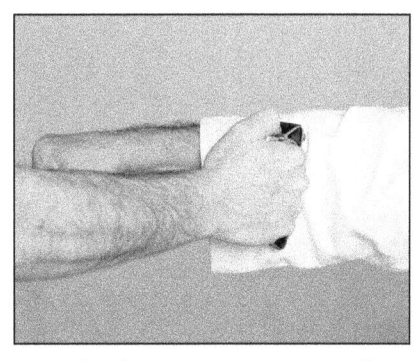 *your thumb on top of the handle; the counterstrike is aimed at the opponent's arm (i.e., elbow, wrist, or hand—see detail shown above).* **2c)** Press with the right tekko to unbalance the opponent and move his arm away. *Key point*: *When you press with the tekko make sure to do it in a snapping action.* **2d)** Shift your weight onto your right leg, slide in and deliver a high, left vertical punch. *Key point: The punch must be performed vertically with the thumb stabilizing the tekko.*

Asian Martial Arts • Practical Applications

# Mantis Boxing

Ilya Profatlov, M.A.

Mantis boxing, an elegant yet highly practical branch of Chinese martial arts, has been the driving force in my life for the last twenty years. That is why I have dedicated a good part of the last decade to collecting and preserving the history and practice of the style. This extended research project has yielded a wealth of information, as well as an extended repertoire of useful combat techniques. One such technique, called *taiji da*, or grand ultimate striking, quickly became one of my favorites. Taiji da has proven to be very effective throughout history, and practicing this technique can greatly benefit any martial artist.

Five years ago, my research landed me deep in the heart of Shandong peninsula, the place where Mantis Boxing was first created. By this time, I had already spent a great deal of time interviewing great masters and learning their forms of Plum Blossom Mantis Boxing (*Meihua Tanglang Quan*), the oldest recorded style of Mantis gongfu. Since I launched my research project in 1999, many masters had already grown old and died off, and I felt that my window of opportunity was coming to an end. After several fruitless trips to China, I was ready to give in to despondency, when a chance happening led me to visit one last village, Yuan Niu of Haiyang County. It was there that I found Lin Tangfang (林棠芳, 1920–2009), a master of Plum Blossom Mantis Boxing with skills that left me awestruck. He accepted me as a disciple and taught me his time-tested fighting system, including the invaluable principles of taiji da.

Taiji da (太極打) can best be described as a line of progression in close-range fighting. The principle of taiji da prepares the fighter to react to any number of close-range combat situations with speed and precision. Individual Plum Blossom fighting techniques can be combined in sets of three to five applications. Through the diligent practice of all Plum Blossom fighting techniques, and by applying them in logical sequences, the mantis practitioner can confidently surmount even the most menacing adversary. Nearly two hundred years ago, Liang Xuexiang (梁學香, 1810–1895) recorded in his boxing manuals a concise poem that outlines the style:

The transformations of mantis boxing are endless,
Mantis hands, cold rooster stance, plum blossom body, grand ultimate strikes,
Mantis hands have tens of thousands of changes,
In cold rooster stance, the plum blossom opens into five petals.

This poem emphasizes the importance of rigorously training basic stances and hand techniques. Once all that is up to speed, taiji da can be achieved through masterful combinations (see next pages).

Grandmaster Lin Tangfang used taiji da throughout his life to establish himself as a famous and unbeatable fighter. In his youth, Lin used these techniques to nobly protect his village from Japanese invaders during World War II. He trained the village militia in Plum Blossom Mantis techniques, and they successfully warded off the Japanese in both armed and open-hand combat. When Lin reached his late eighties, he retained every bit of his fighting spirit and ability. One day, eighty-seven-year-old Lin was out on a quiet morning walk when he was confronted by a much younger man. This man said he was looking for the infamous Lin Tangfang, in order to test his boxing skills. Lin smiled and, in order to be humble, told the man that the master had died long ago, but he was his gongfu brother. He calmly challenged the man to test his skills. The man lunged at Lin, who instantaneously met his strike with a solid taiji da. With two ironlike fingers, the old master effortlessly knocked out the man's front teeth and went on his way.

Taiji da has proven time and time again to be a highly effective principle. Through practice and determination, the use of taiji da can elevate any fighter to a new level.

The late Grandmaster Lin Tangfang (1919–2009).

## Techniques: Taiji Da Combinations

When the opponent strikes (1), one must shift away from the line of attack and intercept with a double-blocking strike. The left hand acts as a soft, assisting grab, and the right hand acts as a hard block. The right hand immediately strikes the opponent in the jaw with the wrist (2). If the opponent blocks (3), one can pull the opponent downward (4), either unbalancing him or causing him to pull back. If the opponent pulls back, one can follow and hit the opponent hard in the neck with the right straight palm (5).

If the opponent blocks that last strike (6), one can press down on the hand and use the left "sneaking hand" to grab the opponent's wrist (7), simultaneously applying pressure on his elbow and placing the right foot on the inside of the opponent's left ankle (8). As the hands deliver the strike, one must use the right leg to deliver a solid bump to the opponent's left leg, and then sweep him diagonally to the right (9). One must take this opportunity to attack the opponent until he is immobilized (10).

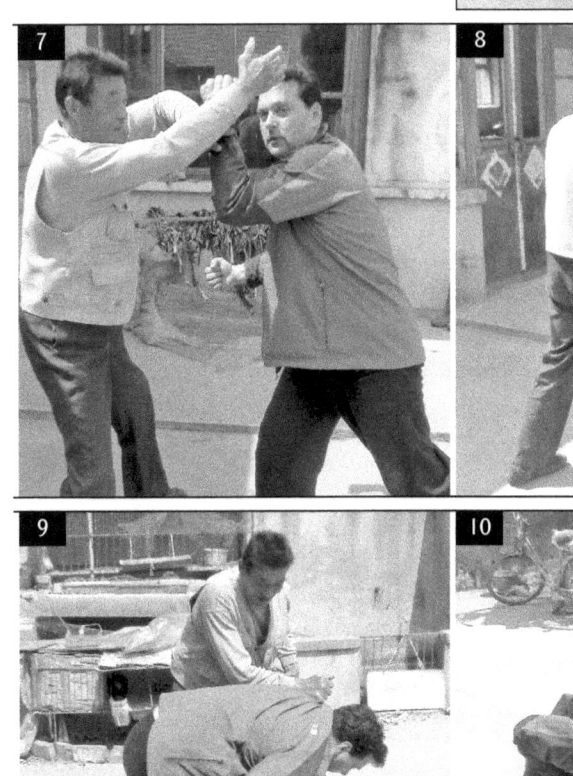

# Combat Systema

Kevin Secours, B.Ed.

### Where I Learned These Techniques

I first encountered the idea of the Russian two-on-one arm tie during my early years of jujutsu in my teens. My teacher introduced it as a favorite of Russian wrestlers and emphasized how strong it is for keeping control of the attacker's arm while keeping your own body on the outside of the attacker. I gained a much deeper appreciation of the tactic some years later, when I was training it with some colleagues who were hardcore into Sambo and then of course, saw it again in Systema practice, before truly appreciating the spectrum of options from this position.

### Memorable Incidents Involving These Techniques

The two-on-one always had a place in my arsenal, but when I was working the door at a club, I got overtaken while clearing up an altercation in the bathroom. I ended up on my back on the floor between the toilet and the wall of the stall, piston kicking upward to keep away a patron away who was obviously high on something and speed stabbing with a knife. A colleague ended up coming to my aid and started pulling him off of me, but the space was so tight and the guy was so cranked up that he wasn't changing his focus. I ended up getting a grip on the knife hand with both hands and literally climbed my way back up onto my knees as my teammate ripped out his legs and took him down. It took a lot more work to subdue him, but I never let go of his arm after that. I had another blade encounter on the job over a year later, and I went to the two-on-one by default and drove the attacker hard into the wall. I kept control of him for a minute until I realized he was out on impact. The penny dropped for me then and I started seriously studying how to integrate this technique and have seen incredible results in my students ever since.

### Tips on Practicing These Techniques

Like anything else, give yourself time. A lot of people feel a lot more comfortable striking than grappling, but in my experience, boxing a knife is suicide in some situations. Sometimes there is absolutely nowhere to move and if you can get a solid grip on the knife hand, you can prevent your attacker from retracting the blade easily and interrupt his flow.

It's important to practice the tactic from various types of grabs. In sequence 1, I have shown a nape grab where the attacker is trying to pull you into the knife. In these cases, I've found it's easier to blend with the weapon and to latch on to the knife hand. In sequence 2, I am being held strongly from the front and kept at the attacker's ideal distance. In this situation, it's very tough to reach and control the knife hand and it's generally easier, although admittedly somewhat counterintuitive, to attack the free hand. Drilling these types of variations is pivotal for developing a feel for the energy behind the attack.

When shielding against the knife, use whatever works for you. I tend to prefer offering the outside of my forearm, since it's more durable than the inside. It also reduces the tendency to snatch with the fingers and forces you to go deeper into the deflection. This allows me to follow the knife hand back on its retraction path and lets me divert even very powerful counter stabs with the ramp created by my frame. Having your second hand ready in a high frame position is very useful for checking the hand if it veers high, and it helps thwart a clinch fight from breaking out.

Beyond that, the key is to apply constant pressure. Meet the knife hand and drive with the full force of your body. Spear the crown of your head into the attacker's face, drive his knife hand into his hips and groin, and absolutely destroy the attacker's thighs with knee strikes as you run forward. It is essential to "attack the attacker," to switch his mindset from predator to desperate survivor and to fixate on prevailing and continuing at any cost once you have engaged. Once you've acquired the two-on-one, you can wrench the arm a number of different ways or even go for locks, but I tend to favor simple manipulations like ripping the attacker forward to the triangulation point. As two-legged creatures, we are forever in a state of imbalance, seeking that invisible third point that would grant us the perfect stability of a tripod. By pulling your attacker sharply on a 45-degree angle toward this triangulation point, you can steal his balance with minimal effort and destroy his weapon hand on the ground in the process. From there, you can decide whether you want to end it standing or steer the attacker to the ground according to your preference.

## Technique 1

**1a)** The attacker grabs you by the nape and rushes in with a flurry of quick slashes. You move inside the power line, greeting the knife hand with the outside of your nearest forearm. Keep your second hand ready on the highline to counter any sudden changes in trajectory.

**1b)** You check the knife hand with your free arm, driving it powerfully into the attacker with the full power of your hips as he attempts to retract the weapon and reset for another attack.

**1c)** As the attacker's knife hand rebounds toward you with another stab, you hook underneath his elbow with a movement akin to an uppercut punch, jamming the back of his joint with the inner crook of your own elbow. This can jam the joint and will prevent further retraction. Train yourself to catch the knife hand at the wrist with your right hand almost immediately after securing the elbow.

**1d)** Maintaining this control on the knife arm with both hands, drive forward into the attacker, blitzing his thigh with painful low-line knee strikes and disrupting his balance and rhythm.

**1e)** Then, sliding your left hand down alongside your right to seize the attacker's wrist with a baseball-bat grip, step forward, dropping your full weight towards your attacker's triangle point and driving his knife hand into the ground. Be careful not to lose your own balance in the process. Stay balanced and snap back slightly before you make contact with your hands to prevent mishaps with the blade.

## Technique 2

**2a)** If your attacker grabs you from the front of the body with the intent of pushing you away, it is difficult to access his knife hand.

**2c)** With the full power and speed of your hips, turn your torso sharply back toward the attacker as he falls in toward you, and clamp your hands around his face and head like a bear trap. The goal should be to rend and crush his soft tissue immediately and to torque his head back to the right. This jarring action can swing the knife hand away from you. Often, this combined shock will cause an attacker to drop the weapon.

**2b)** Instead, turn the full mass of your body in toward the back of his elbow joint, hyperextending the joint of his free arm. This can be done simply by the motion of your body. Here, the author has maintained control of the sleeve of the attacker's jacket to keep him closer and to amplify the damage to the joint.

**2d)** To bring the attacker to the ground, sharply twist his head back in the opposite direction, stepping back with your left leg slightly to make room for his stumble. You can control the head or make this fall as violent as you wish. The attacker's flailing knife hand can be caught and trapped with the wing of your armpit, providing a powerful control. You may wish to resort to joint locks, destructions or hits to finish.

# Modern Arnis

Ken Smith

**Where I Learned These Techniques**

The two techniques I've selected as favorites are the center lock with cane, and a technique we'll simply refer to as "left-hand technique number 1." I practiced and refined these techniques under the tutelage of the late Grandmaster Remy Presas. But my initial introduction to each of these techniques came at the hands of other arnisadors: center lock with cane was introduced to me by his first arnis teacher, George Mazek, although it was not until sometime later that I came to appreciate the full power of this technique. Likewise, it was Chuck Gauss who first introduced me to left-hand technique number 1, which many people recognize as Professor Presas's go-to technique in almost any situation. As a result, it is fair to say that this second technique was a favorite of Gauss as well.

**Memorable Incidents Involving These Techniques**

One of the wonderful things about having the opportunity to train directly with the headmaster of a system is being able to learn by feeling. Every student can see the master performing the technique and hear his verbal instructions, but only the student with whom the technique is being demonstrated can actually feel the move. This experience serves to convey nuances that simply elude detection by the other senses. In this respect, I was fortunate to be a favorite choice of partner for Professor Presas when demonstrating a technique. And while I had learned the center lock with cane some time before, it was not until a seminar in Michigan with Professor Presas in the early 1990s that I experienced its full effect. Rather than simply induce localized pain in my wrist, the application of the lock by Professor Presas—while not unduly rough—caused a shock reaction that extended beyond his wrist, affecting my entire body. This kind of hands-on experience provides lessons of incomparable value for those who strive to attain true mastery of their chosen art.

One of the most important teachings in any martial art is that techniques must be performed with the right mind-set. This is especially important when dealing with set-up techniques, fakes, or feints. Unless the opponent truly believes the initial move is being executed in earnest, he will not be drawn into the behavior it is intended to elicit. Worse still, if the opponent recognizes the feint as a hollow threat, he will have a window to launch his own attack with impunity. It will, in essence, give him a free shot. With this teaching in mind, one of the more memorable aspects of performing left-hand technique number 1 is the way in which the initial counter—while planned to set up for the next move—will often reach its target unchecked if the opponent is not quick and alert, thereby obviating the need for the rest of the sequence. In this way, the set-up technique may actually become the finishing technique if executed with the proper mind-set.

### Tips on Practicing the Center Lock with Cane
- When performing the center lock with cane, the practitioner should employ a "tapi-tapi block." Unlike the more basic "post block," where the defender blocks using his cane but braces it on the rear side with his palm, in executing the tapi-tapi block, the cane blocks the cane and the arm blocks the arm.
- When the opponent attacks, the defender must ensure that the angle of his cane matches the angle of the striking cane, otherwise the canes may miss one another.
- Similarly, in executing the cane block, the defender must avoid crossing the centerline with his weapon. Failing to follow this rule may cause the block to make contact but then collapse.
- When the defender grasps his opponent's cane, his pinky finger should touch the opponent's thumb so he can detect his opponent's grip by feel.

### Tips on Practicing Left-Hand Technique Number 1
- In performing left-hand technique number 1, it is important to note that after executing a tapi-tapi block in response to his opponent's strike, the defender counters not just with the right backfist, but also with a simultaneous left jab to the opponent's stomach with the tip of the cane. This additional, simultaneous attack is easy to miss if you are not looking for it.
- After the opponent accepts the "invitation" to parry the backfist and goes to strike the defender with his cane a second time, the defender must step forward and out to the side with his left leg in order to "counter the counter" effectively. This footwork will reorient the angle of engagement, creating a new centerline for the defender while forcing the attacker to cross his own centerline, thereby weakening him enough to allow the defender's (grabbed) right arm to overpower the opponent's left (grabbing) arm.

### Technique 1: Center Lock with Cane

1a) The attacker backhand strikes at shoulder level with a cane. 1b) The defender blocks with his own cane and controls the attacking arm with his left hand. 1c) The defender slides his empty hand onto his opponent's cane and pulls it toward himself while striking at the opponent's ear with the butt end of his own cane, inviting the opponent to parry. 1d) When the opponent parries, the defender pushes the opponent's cane tip down over the opponent's wrist, and locks it in place with his cane. He then pins the opponent's open hand on his wrist to apply the center lock. 1e) The defender finishes with a strike to the face while bracing the opponent's head with his other hand.

## Technique 2: Left-Hand Technique Number 1

**2a)** The attacker strikes at shoulder level with his cane. **2b)** The defender blocks the strike with his cane and controls the opponent's hand with his right hand. **2c)** The defender immediately strikes with a right backfist to the attacker's head, inviting a block while the tip of his cane simultaneously strikes the opponent's stomach. **2d)** The attacker parries the backfist down and retracts his cane to strike again. **2e)** The defender changes his stance and angle, forcing the attacker to cross his centerline. He parries the attacker's second strike, and counterstrikes to his head to end the sequence.

# Jujutsu and Judo

Nicklaus Suino, J.D.

### Where I Learned These Techniques

I've been lucky to train with a few superlative martial artists, and the techniques featured here are a synthesis of movements taught in two closely related Japanese arts: the self-defense techniques of Nihon Jujutsu taught by the late Sato Shizuya (1929–2011), and an approach to judo that I was first exposed to by Tabata Sensei, who taught at the Kanagawa Kenritsu Budokan.

We trained with Sato at the dojo in the American Embassy Compound. In Sato's self-defense methods, there's a defense against a rear collar grab that involves suddenly turning toward your attacker, overwhelming his balance, and executing a major outside reap (*osotogari*). In that technique, the pull by the attacker creates momentum that can be used against him in a very dynamic manner. In my favorite approach to osotogari, I face my opponent and I create the momentum by pushing.

Tabata was the consummate finesse judo player. He was supremely strong and endowed with extraordinary judo intelligence. He routinely called his throws before executing them. Despite these warnings, I found myself airborne on a regular basis.

One of Tabata's hallmark methods was what I have come to call "momentum judo," wherein he would amplify the power of a push or pull by swinging one leg. Employing his hips as a fulcrum, he would transmit the power of the leg into his upper body to take over my balance. Because his arms were relaxed, and because his power came from momentum rather than from his being rooted to the mat, it was very difficult to resist. The second technique shown in this article is a modified side wheel (*yoko guruma*) applied when a partner recoils after being pulled forward.

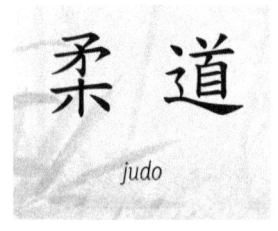

*judo*

### Memorable Incidents Involving These Techniques

If you've practiced judo, you know it's an art that keeps you humble. You can rest assured that for every glorious throw I've managed to catch, I've been thrown a few dozen times by better judo players.

At our dojo, we have a judo black belt who goes by the nickname "Doctor Ippon." His real name is John Kuchinski and he is totally blind. Despite his blindness, he has an explosive one-arm back carry throw (*ippon seoinage*) that can surprise even the most seasoned judo player.

A few months ago, Doctor Ippon and I were engaging in a vigorous round of randori. A moment came in our sparring session when John stepped back and I was able to swing my outside leg forward, snap all the slack out of our arms, and enter for a gigantic outside reap. I was as dumbfounded as he was. The astonished look on his face as he cartwheeled through the air was priceless. There had been virtually no effort on my part and the resultant output of energy was ten times greater than that I had put in.

John expressed his surprise and approval in terms I'd rather not repeat here. But he added, "That was the coolest thing that's ever happened to me!"

Another of our judo addicts is Jonathan Zwicker, a professor of Japanese studies at the University of Michigan. Last summer Jonathan had just returned from a month in Tokyo, where he had attended a week-long judo camp at the Kodokan. He was disporting himself with his usual vigor when I noticed he was sliding his right leg back each time he moved to his rear. I was able to get him to repeat the motion by pulling him strongly forward, then releasing. I swung myself toward him while dropping to the mat, pushing his right leg into his left leg and sending him suddenly and forcefully to the floor.

**Tips on Practicing These Techniques**

The key to both of these techniques is learning to let go of the feeling of being rooted to the floor. Momentum judo requires a willingness to float so that the energy created by the struggle of randori is supplemented by leverage and gravity. We practice adding momentum by swinging one leg either toward or away from the direction the combatants are moving.

For example, I will push my training partner away and, when he reaches the end of my outstretched arms, I'll swing one leg forward. My lower body swings forward and, because I am pivoting at the hips, my upper body swings backward. The energy is transmitted to my partner through my arms, which act like ropes connecting our shoulders. If your partner goes with the motion, you can apply a throw that continues forward, such as a whirling throw (*tomoenage*). If he pulls back, you charge in for osotogari.

If you swing your leg backward (pulling your partner forward) and he resists by pulling back, watch to see if his forward leg slides back. If it does, you can swing through it with a modified side wheel (yoko guruma).

**Technique 1: Momentum Osotogari**

1a) Step into your partner to push him back. 1b) Swing your leg forward and, pivoting at the hips, let your shoulders swing back to take all the slack out of your arms. 1c) Continue the leg swing with a big move toward the outside rear corner. 1d) Swing your following leg forward, using the momentum to pull your partner toward you. 1e) Execute a major outside reap, cutting out the near leg of your partner and dropping him.

**Technique 2: Momentum Yoko Guruma**

**2a)** Step away from your partner to get the slack out of your arms. **2b)** Forcefully pull your partner's shoulders forward by swinging your leg back. **2c)** When your partner tries to regain an upright posture, step aggressively forward. **2d)** Drop to the floor while bringing your following leg strongly into your partner's retreating leg. You're floating at this point, with both feet sliding forward rather than planted. Execute a modified side wheel, cutting out the lead leg of your partner and dropping him.

# Niten Ichi-ryu and Shinto-ryu

Kim Taylor, M.Sc.

The techniques discussed here come from two different schools of Japanese sword, and from two of the most important instructors for me personally and for Canadian *iaido* (a sword art) and *jodo* (use of short staff). Haruna Matsuo (1925–2002) taught the classical sword system of Niten Ichi-ryu to a few students for several years, beginning in the early 1990s.

The technique called *aisen* (合先), which I present here, came to represent the essence of Miyamoto Musashi's (c. 1584–1645) sword style for me. Direct, no-nonsense, and almost arrogant, this technique requires much confidence and not a little courage to perform. It is the final technique of a set demonstrating techniques of short sword against a long sword.

Upon learning that some of us were studying jodo, Haruna introduced us to Namitome Shigenori. Namitome was chair of the jodo section for the All Japan Kendo Federation. On a visit to Japan a few years back, we spent some time practicing in Namitome's dojo and he consented to teach us the twelve katas of Shinto-ryu sword techniques.

The technique *tsuki dachi* (突出 thrusting stance) is the final short-sword kata and final kata of the set that includes eight long-sword and four short-sword techniques. The technique has many similarities to aisen. Like Musashi, Muso Gonnosuke Katsuyoshi (c. 605) was not a little arrogant, as this technique seems to indicate to me. There is no trick here, no evasion. One offers a target and then takes it away. Miss the timing or the distance and you are dealing with an injury.

One memory involving aisen from Niten Ichi-ryu would be the amused look on Haruna's face when he demonstrated this to me for the first time: one moment I was swinging to strike through his undefended head, and the next the tip of his short sword was touching my throat, my own sword useless beside his knee and my expression obviously one of open-mouthed amazement.

The most memorable incident for tsuki dachi is the day I learned the technique in Namitome's dojo, with its red pine floors dented to golf-ball consistency by years of stick and sword hits. The light from the afternoon sun coming in through floor-level windows reflected from the wood in thousands of points, while a breeze through the bamboo grove behind the building made a sound I will never forget. Laughter, sweat and fear—the most delightful combination one can experience during a career in the martial arts.

Aisen and tsuki dachi both require the swordsman to stay directly on the attack line through the entire technique. Because of this, the opponent must be controlled by giving him a single irresistible target and the swordsman must have the patience to wait until the opponent has committed his swing toward that target. Once this happens, there is little time to react and defeat him. Fear must not be allowed to tighten muscles and delay the movements. Everything is bet on a single swing and response. There is no room for error or adjustment. They either work or they do not.

By offering your head or your hand, you must control the opponent's actions. He must believe he has no choice but to swing at the targets offered. If he thinks you will not simply run him over should he fail to attack, the technique will fail. Total commitment to the kata is required to make these techniques real.

Aisen begins by placing the short sword (*shoto*) edge down across the chest at shoulder height. This position seems completely open to attack. The swordsman walks directly toward the opponent and lets him swing. As the opponent swings at the swordsman's head, the swordsman closes his hand and extends his arm to sweep the sword off the attack line to his left side. After striking aside the sword, the swordsman rotates the shoto in his hand and thrusts into the throat of the opponent. In order to do this properly, the swordsman must wait until the opponent is committed to his attack, and then attack into it. In order to sweep the sword to the side, the shoto must sweep down the long sword's side. The most difficult skill is to adjust the pacing toward the opponent so that even if he does cut down, he will only skim the forehead of the swordsman. This lets the short sword strike the long sword at its weakest part, near the tip, where it is moving fastest. Aisen is a *sen no sen* timing—the swordsman attacks into the attack.

Tsuki dachi begins with the swordsman holding the shoto, edge to his left, directly in line with the opponent's throat and approaching boldly. If the opponent does not react, the swordsman must have the intent to thrust through the opponent's throat. Seeing this intent, the opponent will strike the shoto or the swordsman's right hand away before attacking on his own behalf. As the strike is made to his exposed hand, the swordsman snaps it away and then strikes down on the wrist of the opponent before he can recover. Like aisen, patience is demanded of this technique until the opponent commits fully to the strike. Taking the target away and striking into the opening created by the failed attack takes relaxed and unwavering movement. Tsuki dachi is a *go no sen*—an avoidance of the attack and a counterattack into weakness.

## Technique 1: Aisen

1a) Hold the short sword in this position across the chest, the hand lightly open with the fingers ready to snap the blade to your left.

1b) Approach the opponent directly in a normal walking position, hips square to the front.

1c) Snap the short sword to the left, pivoting on the wrist. Do not move the right hand toward the centerline until after you have struck the sword aside. Do not move to either side of the attack line.

1d) Move the right hand to the centerline while turning the short sword so it is now edge to the right with your palm down. Move directly and strongly forward into the opponent to thrust his throat. Your feet will be together at this point.

## Technique 2: Tsuki Dachi

2a) Raise the short sword to your own throat height and hold it parallel to the ground, aimed at the opponent's throat.

2b) Approach within attack range of the opponent with the full intent of running him through.

2c) When the opponent strikes at your attacking hand, pull your right foot back to your left and at the same time swing the shoto up and to the side.

2d) Keeping the wrist in the same position, use your whole arm as your "sword" and strike down on the opponent's right wrist as you move your own right foot forward again into attack range.

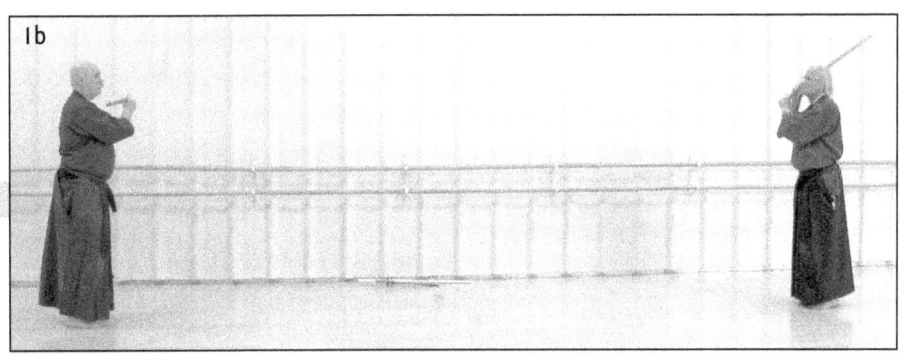

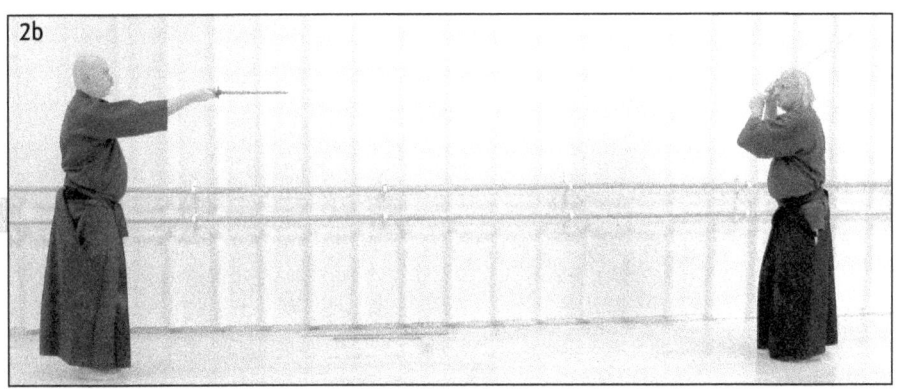

# Ving Tsun Double-Knives

Jeff Webb

Two weapon sets taught in Ving Tsun gongfu are the long-staff set known in Cantonese as *luk-dim-boon-gwun* (Mandarin *liudian ban gun fa*, 六點半棍法, meaning six-and-a-half-point pole) and the double-knives set called *bart-cham-do* in Cantonese (Mandarin: *ba zhan dao*, 八斬刀, meaning eight cutting blades). Considered advanced instruction, these are taught only to practitioners who have already mastered the empty-hand aspects of the system.

As a former student of Grandmaster Leung Ting, the closed-door disciple of the late Grandmaster Yip Man, I consider myself fortunate to have studied the weapons under his instruction and additionally with some of my gongfu brothers. It is well known that Yip Man highly regarded the double-knives techniques and taught the whole form to not more than four people in his lifetime. Among these, Leung is widely regarded as his most accomplished student in this area.

Owing to the somewhat exclusive nature of Ving Tsun weapons training and to the itinerant lifestyle of my former teacher, each lesson on the weapons was a memorable one. As a general rule, lessons on the weapons were always private or at least semiprivate in nature. Over the years, my weapons instruction took place in no less than six different cities and at venues ranging from martial arts schools to hotel rooms and balconies.

Yet my fondest memories are of my very first weapons lesson, which took place in San Antonio, Texas, back in 1988. At that time, my gongfu brother Gilbert Leal was hosting a general seminar by our teacher and had invited a select few to attend an additional session that was held afterward. The topic was the double-knives routine.

Though we were only taught one practice sequence that day (shown in photos 1a–5a), it was a rare opportunity and therefore the most meaningful for a young student. Only years later, when I formally learned the weapons, would I realize these movements were derived from the first two sections of the double-knives form. The sequence shown in photos 1b–5b is an application of movements from the fifth section of the form.

In the double-knives set, as in empty-hand Ving Tsun, good footwork is essential. Beyond being merely a delivery system for our techniques, Ving Tsun footwork is a method of moving the body as a unit to augment the execution of those techniques. Therefore, the double-knives set places great emphasis on coordinating the knife movements with body shifting and momentum for both offensive and defensive gain.

A practical example of this is the knife technique used to deal with long weapons. When facing an opponent armed with a long pole or a spear, the knife practitioner will employ advanced footwork to quickly bridge the gap and get in close. At this short range, the enemy's longer weapon is rendered unwieldy and thus is a disadvantage. For this reason, footwork practice is at the top of the list when it comes to improving your proficiency with the double-knives set. In addition, the following three areas are important:

▶ **Correct Mindset:** Weapons training must be approached with the proper mindset. The weapons techniques were developed during a historical period when real combat skills meant the difference between life and death. In Ving Tsun there is a saying: "Fear the younger opponent in fist fighting; fear the older [more experienced] opponent in weapons fighting." Being struck during an empty-hand fight is not necessarily fatal, but in weapons fighting, every blow landed is potentially crippling, if not lethal. Therefore, weapons practice should always be performed with a serious attitude.

▶ **Realistic Practice:** Once the movements can be performed at normal speed, one should begin practicing them with increasing speed and power. This extends to both the forms training and the practical applications against an opponent. Defending against weapons at walk-through pace is not enough; training at functional speed is essential to developing functional skills.

▶ **Repetition, Repetition, Repetition:** Upon beginning my formal weapons training in early 2002, my teacher said something that has stuck with me ever since. He said that all too often, after a student has learned the weapons, that student spends little actual time practicing them. For many, the prestige of acquiring the weapons knowledge is more important than practicing and getting good at them. The one notable exception was his senior European student, Keith R. Kernspecht, whom he candidly stated was his best student of the weapons, owing to Kernspecht's long-term, continual practice. It should be obvious that facility and expertise come not from just a few hundred repetitions, but from thousands.

Improving one's skills at anything in life can be done by applying these same principles. Approach things with a correct mindset, practice in a realistic fashion, and above all remember that it takes repetition to make the master.

**Technique 1**

**1a)** Jeff Webb faces an opponent armed with a wooden bat. **1b)** As the opponent steps in and swings, Webb steps forward at an angle, simultaneously contacting the attacker's hand and throat with the "dragging knives" (*tal-do*) technique. **1c–e)** Webb quickly follows up with the chain stabbing technique to the torso.

1a

1b

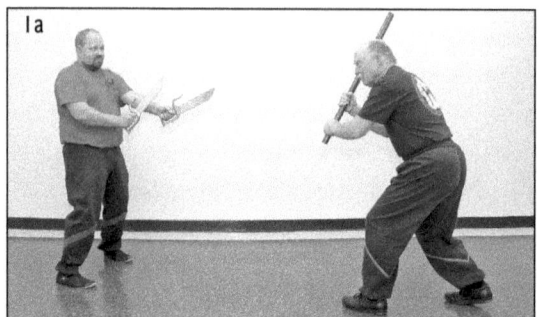

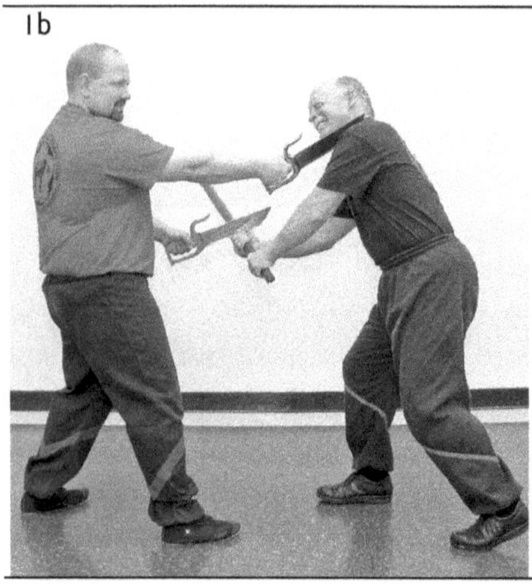

1c

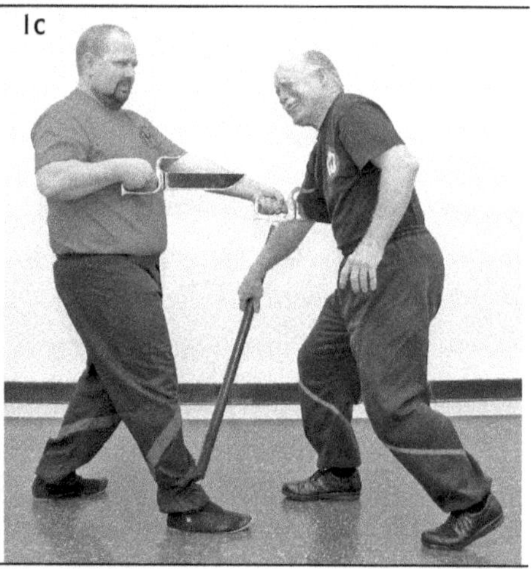

1d

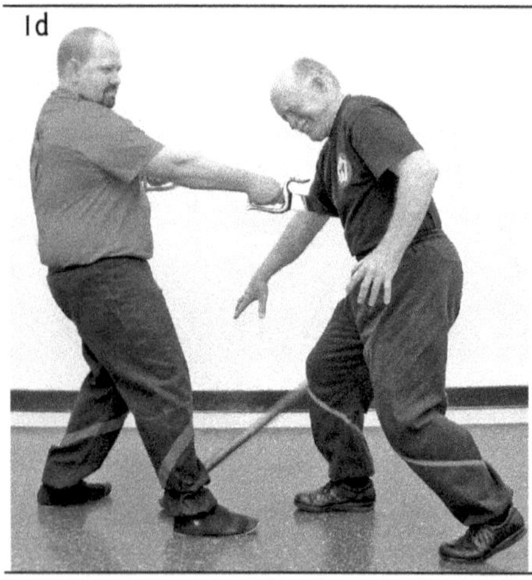

1e

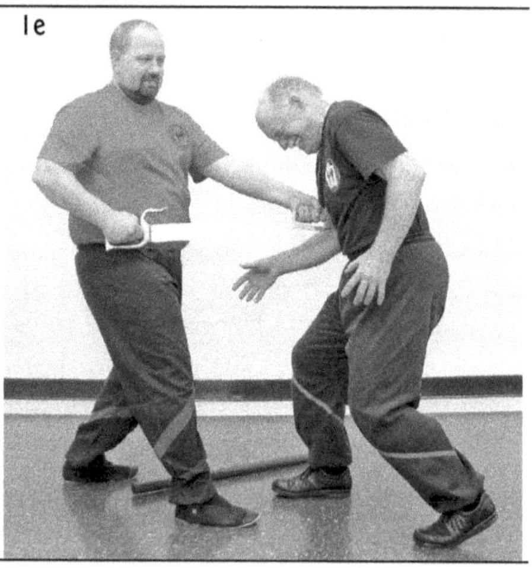

## Technique 2

**2a)** Webb faces an opponent wielding a heavy machete. **2b)** As the attacker swings downward, Webb makes contact with the "asking knife" (*man-do*) technique. **2c)** Guiding the machete past him as he advances, Webb counters with a "throat-cutting knife" (*shat-geng-do*) technique. **2d)** The attacker drops his weapons and collapses, but not before receiving additional stabbing attacks to the torso.

Asian Martial Arts • Practical Applications

# Bajiquan

Tony Yang

When I first started martial arts with the late Liu Yunqiao (劉雲樵 1909–1992), I had already spent many years training in the various systems of northern Praying Mantis. My first encounter with Bajiquan left me with the impression that it seemed far too simple in appearance and movement to be effective against the quickness and speed of a complex system like Praying Mantis. However, I was shocked to see a very skilled Praying Mantis practitioner attempt to quickly launch an attack into Liu only to find himself thrown back ten feet in a matter of seconds. Liu accomplished this with minimal body movement. From that day on, I knew something of greater substance was operating below the surface appearance of Bajiquan.

My descent into the depths of the Baji system took many years of foundational training, starting with the basic Baji-style horse stance and endless hours of postlike stance training. Through this step-by-step process of development, I finally began to understand how Baji's simplistic external appearance is supported by a deeply aligned structure of internal strength and stillness. Every punch, elbow strike, and shoulder strike mobilizes full-body utilization. The characteristic external explosiveness of Baji emanates from a deep source of stillness and returns to that same stillness. It is something expressed in Liu's calligraphy, but also something I had never experienced in all of my previous martial arts training. I found that qi, neigong, meditation, and five-phase theory (*wuxing*) now made experiential practical sense. Prior to this, it was like trying to capture the experience of eating a gourmet meal by reading the recipe and cooking instructions.

Now, achieving this level of understanding and skill did not come easily and took great effort and discipline in internal and external training methods: stance training while maintaining inner calmness and relaxed breathing; big spear (*da qiang*) training with relaxed intent and full-body extension, utilization, and coordinated breathing; post/tree training and general two-person training with great body awareness and sensitivity. Systematic and quite deep, it was well beyond anything I had ever dreamed a martial art could be.

The first technique we see illustrated is called "fierce tiger climbs the mountain." It was the favorite practice of both Li Shuwen (李書文 1864–1934) and his younger protégé, Liu Yunqiao. In this application, every part of the body is systematically committed until the opponent is destroyed. It illustrates a folding principle of fist to elbow, elbow to shoulder, and ends with a horizontal, upward blow to the kidney (1a through 1d, demonstrated by Tony Yang and James Finley). The open-hand techniques of this application can be mapped and trained to specific big spear techniques. This is necessary in order to develop full-body utilization, power, and effectiveness in the open-hand strikes.

The second technique illustrated is "large wrap" (*da chan*) (2a through 2d, demonstrated by Tony Yang and James Finley). This technique not only requires full-body utilization to generate its power, but also requires great physical sensitivity when bridging the spatial gap. Timing is critical, since this sensitivity is the engine leading the power train.

I once had a student who was well over six feet tall and very skilled in the art of Taekwondo. He asked to try me in a very serious way. When he attempted to deliver a high kick, I employed a variation of the da chan technique. He said he felt my shoulder strike his chest area, and the next thing he knew, he was lying on the ground, desperately gasping for air. He swore this was because he was struck in the chest, but he also complained about the pain in his groin and could not figure out how this had happened. What he failed to realize was that when I struck his chest area, he also was being simultaneously hit in the lower abdomen and groin/testicles. My arm, shoulder, outside forearm, and hand were employed at the exact same time. It was as though the center of his body, i.e., the top of his chest to the bottom of his testicles, walked into a moving cornered edge of a wall. That blending of timing, softness, hardness, and full-body utilization was something he had never encountered in his martial arts experience. He was quite intrigued by the intricacies of the movements, and also because he had no idea how to train for this type of power.

Our line of Bajiquan (Li Shuwen→Liu Yunqiao→Tony Yang) is a systematic blend of stillness and explosive power, a unified expression of yin and yang principles in the service of full-body utilization. Liu used to tell me that for every minute I stood in a Baji-style horse stance, my life would be extended by a minute. It did not dawn on me until many years later that this had implications well beyond health and longevity. What he was saying was that this very simple-looking stance was the foundational source of stillness, relaxation, and internal strength that would further my martial effectiveness and resonate throughout my higher Bajiquan levels of development. The external explosive power so characteristic of our Baji would start and return to that stillness—and without it, no technique or application would ever realize its completeness and full effectiveness.

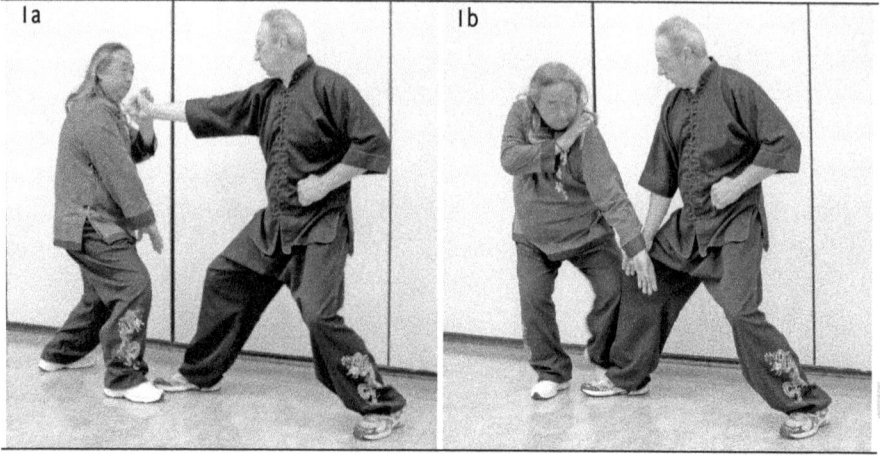

**Technique 1: Large Wrap**

1a) Tony Yang blocks the initial punch by James Finley.

1b) While controlling Finley's right arm, Yang starts stepping into Finley's center.

*Photography by Meissa Lilley.*

**Technique 2: Fierce Tiger Climbs the Mountain**

2a) Tony Yang blocks the initial punch by James Finley.

2b) Immediately following the block is a straight punch to the heart.

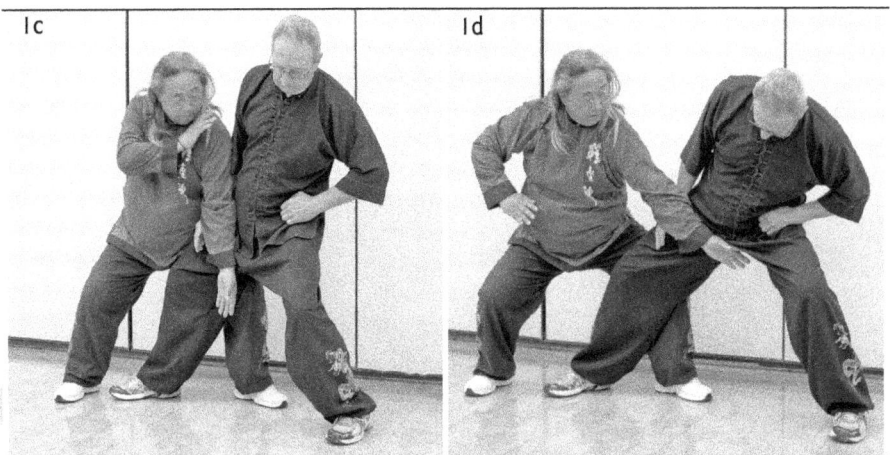

**1c)** Yang's "shoulder strike" (*kao*) actually runs from the shoulder through the arm and extends to his hand. It is one entire movement striking the opponent's inside centerline, from chest to groin, in one simultaneous blow.

**1d)** The last position also sets up any number of movements further into the opponent.

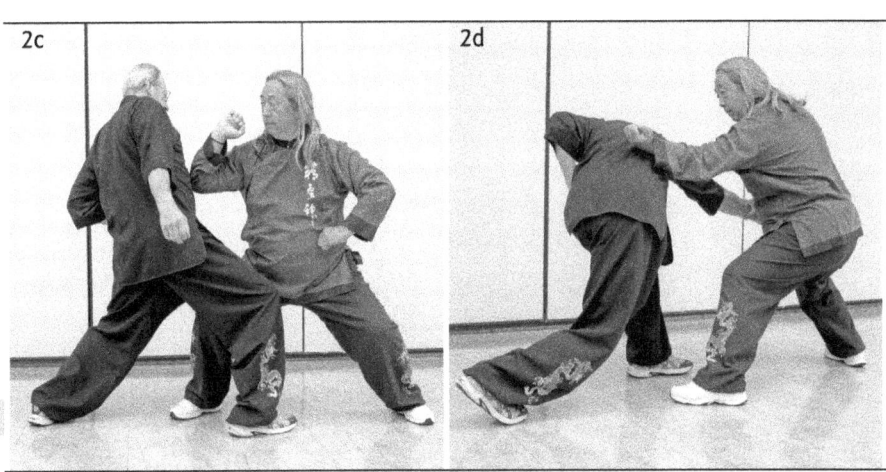

**2c)** The fist strike is immediately followed with an elbow to the heart, then
**2d)** stepping in and finishing with an horizontal/upward strike to the kidney area with the inner part of the forearm. The movement is continuous from start to end and has a subtle but powerful silk-reeling (*chansi jin*) expression.

# Goshin Jutsu and Washin-ryu

Linda Yiannakis, Ph.D.

I learned the Goshin Jutsu and variants from Steve Cunningham at Ju Nan Shin Martial Arts Academy in Connecticut beginning in 1995. The Washin-ryu Jujutsu techniques are from the Washin-ryu (和真流) syllabus that I learned from Andrew Yiannakis at the University of Connecticut starting in the early 1990s.

Many of the Goshin Jutsu techniques that I learned from Mr. Cunningham appear simple to perform but embody important principles underlying everything we do in judo and jujutsu. As he moved into variants and related jujutsu techniques, it required more study to grasp how they worked and what was actually driving them. In fact, when I first began to study with Cunningham, my head was spinning after every class. The concept of teaching and learning by principles was new to me. I'd had a couple of decades or so of judo and some jujutsu at that point, but no one had ever presented things in quite the same way that Cunningham did.

Mr. Cunningham often presented a principle and then taught a variety of diverse techniques that illustrated that principle. This was a major change for me and other students in the class from the technique-oriented teaching that was familiar to us. It took some time to grasp what he was doing, to follow some of the more complex moves, and to appreciate the depth of understanding that could come from this type of learning. When we finally began to get it, it was like light bulbs going on over the heads of all the senior students.

But early on in our training (well before the light bulb incidents), there was an evening when one of my friends was going to have to miss class. She made me promise to e-mail her and tell her everything I had learned that night. True to my word, I wrote up my summary of what I'd learned. I share that summary with you here so that you too can benefit from my sophisticated understanding of that time:

Hello Sharon,

I can tell you all about the self-defense technique. Don't worry, with my expert tutelage it will be just as clear as if you had been there!

▶ **Technique #1**—*Kote Ma Wishy Washy:* Enemy attacks you with right-handed grab, either his right hand or yours, who knows, trying to get your credit card. Twirl madly to the left (or is it the right?), circle his arm up and out, *taisabaki* [reposition] a little, add a pinch of *seoinage* [four-corner throw], and throw him in the opposite direction.

▶ **Technique #2**—*Kote Uke Upsi:* Enemy grabs your wrist, trying to get your watch. Casually and magically slip your hand under his wrist into exactly the lethal spot. Throw. Practice this with seventeen other variants until time for freestyle practice.

▶ **Technique #3**—*Insane Asylum Arm Wrap:* The training partner stupidly tries to punch you in the face. Sidestep with parry and punch that you mystically convert into a *shihonage* [four-direction throw] ... but wait, no it's not! Wrap that arm behind the attacker's head and take him down to the floor. He will be in a straitjacket hold (although he didn't get the jacket on quite right).

So, Sharon, now you can do them as well as I can! Be sure to practice them on your colleagues at school (**Battlefield Principle #43:** Take Away Arm and Enlighten Monkey).

Yours in judo,<br>Linda

The first technique shown on the following pages is a variant of the two-hand grab response in Kodokan Goshin Jutsu. One executes the defense with more rotation than is generally done (1a), using an old forearm twist method (1c), and adds a movement from the second Goshin Jutsu technique (left lapel grab) (1d–e). I chose this because it is a straightforward illustration of several important movement principles. Studying these underlying principles allows techniques to flow smoothly.

The main principles here are as follows: ❶ using the body to power the grip break ❷ using the turn away from the opponent to power the strike, uncoiling the striking arm as you turn back toward the opponent to release this power into the blow; ❸ positioning the arm and wrist properly so that only a small amount of pressure is needed for the lock; and ❹ the alignment of one's hands in front of the body while moving forward from the body's center to raise and control the opponent's arm for the second immobilization.

The second technique shown is from Wa Shin-ryu. You can see some of the same principles in this technique as in the two-hand grab: use of the body's rotation to generate power for the strike (2b), correct positioning for the lock (2d), and centered action throughout.

## Kodokan Goshin Jutsu Two-Hand Grab

1a) Andrew seizes Linda's wrists; she breaks the grip with a strong rotation away. 1b) Linda strikes his temple using the power generated from the previous movement. 1c) She steps back and applies a forearm twist. 1d) Linda drives Andrew's arm up and over, keeping the lock in alignment in front of her center. 1e) She then applies a straight armbar, while also applying pressure through the wrist and into the shoulder.

*Attacker: Andrew Frye*
*Defender: Linda Yiannakis*

## Wa Shin-ryu:
## Elbow Strike and Downward Throw

**2a)** Allen attacks with a straight punch to the midsection.

**2b)** Linda evades by stepping off the line of attack, parries, and powers up the elbow strike with a strong rotation away from Allen.

**2c)** She turns back toward him with an elbow strike.

**2d)** Linda controls Allen's arm in a lock while stepping forward with the outside leg, turning, and driving him back and down.

Many thanks to Sandia Budokan of Albuquerque for allowing us to take these photos at their dojo.

*Attacker: Allen Pittman*
*Defender: Linda Yiannakis*

*Photography by David J. Higgins*

# Taiji Spear

Zhang Yun, M.S.

A famous Chinese martial arts classic said, "Spear is the king of all weapons." The spear was one of the most common and important weapons in ancient times. Compared with other kinds of weapons in its time, the spear was considered powerful because of its length, which made possible faster and more dynamic attacks than any other weapon. On the other hand, when considering spear-on-spear conflict, high level skills are very difficult to master. In the Ming dynasty, traditional spear skills were developed to a high level. In his book *Hands and Arms Journal*, Wu Shu (1610–1695) compared the skills from the most famous spear schools and summarized the features among traditional spear skills. Most of the principles elaborated in Wu's book are still applied in many martial arts groups today.

To learn the spear, the first order of business is to build a solid foundation. In his book, Wu Shu told a story about the importance of basic skills as follows:

> When Wu's teacher Shi Jingyan was young, he and his spear master, Shaolin monk Hongji, the best spear master in the Shaolin Temple at that time, traveled a great deal in order to challenge many masters. They were very confident in their skills and won all of their challenges until one day they met Liu Dechang in Zhending County. When Hongji and Liu fought, after only one touch of their weapons, Liu made Hongji's spear fly from his hands. The experience left Hongji and Shi shaken. The two became Liu's disciples immediately and Liu taught them a few foundation skills. Liu told them that they must practice these skills very hard and carefully for two years.
> 
> Hongji and Shi practiced day by day according to Liu's instruction. After two years, they went back to meet Liu again. Liu was satisfied with their skills and said, "Good. You are done." Hongji and Shi were surprised because they supposed that Liu would teach them more application techniques. But Liu explained to them, "You have already learned many useful techniques before you met me. But your basic skills were not good enough. So this is why I easily won when we fought. Now that your foundation is improved, I do not need to teach you any further techniques; right now you can use all of the techniques which you knew before, but now at a higher level. Just as if you built a house on a poor base, the

building cannot stand well in a hard storm. So I simply rebuilt the base. I do not need to add other materials on other parts of the house. The integrity of the house will now be solid."

Later, both Hongji and Shi became great spear masters. This story tells us the importance of a solid foundation in basic skills, especially for advanced study. It is said that the level you achieve depends on the quality of your foundation. What is a foundation skill? There is a classic poem in answer to this question:

> A warrior holds a golden spear,
> Only uses nine inches' length,
> Draw a circle day by day,
> He can send a good master to meet the king of hell.

Here two technical terms express the meaning of the basic skills of the spear. One is "Only use[s] nine inches' length," which alludes to the skill of thrusting. The other is "Draw a circle day by day," which describes classic spear circling practice. Basic thrusting skill pertains to offense, which should be fast, powerful, and accurate. Circling skill is defense. All blocking and changing techniques come from circles. It is said that even for a successful master, these foundation skills should still be practiced daily throughout life.

Taiji spear inherits all of the principles and skills of traditional spear, as well as employing Taiji philosophy, principles, and skills. Taiji spear employs these principles in order to develop highly efficient abilities and to apply the basic skills of Taijiquan, such as sticking, adhering, following, linking, and so on. These principles and skills make Taiji spear different from other types of spear.

It is said that Taiji empty-hand and spear practice were taught at the Qianzai Temple (千载寺) in the Ming dynasty. Later when Yang Luchan (1799–1872) taught Taiji in Beijing, he passed his spear skills to Wu Quanyou (1834–1902). Then Quanyou taught these skills to Wang Maozhai (1862–1940). Wang also got instruction from a mysterious master Li. Wang Peisheng (1919–2004) learned Taiji with Wang Maozhai from the age of thirteen. Wang Peisheng won a great reputation as a fighter, especially in spear fighting. I was lucky enough to learn Taiji spear with Wang Peisheng starting in 1980.

In the following section, we introduce two techniques of Taiji spear. Both are based on the foundation skill of circling. One is a variation of the foundation skills. The other is based on well-known traditional spear skills with the addition of Taiji features.

## TECHNIQUE 1

### Golden Rooster Pecking—Circling and Pecking

If your opponent attacks you with his spear at midlevel, drop your spearhead downward slightly (**1a**). When the tip of his spear is close to you, turn your spear up in a circle from the right side of his spear (**1b**). As soon as your spear is higher than his, turn your spear down in a circle and make the tip of your spear peck his front hand. It is a hard downward strike. If it hits on his hand directly, it will hurt badly. If he dodges his hand, your spear will still hit the shaft. Both can easily knock his spear from his front hand (**1c**). At this time, the only thing your opponent can do is jump backward to escape, so immediately following this strike, you should step forward to chase and thrust toward him (**1d**). Here the key is that your spear is controlled and moved in a circle from your waist. The spear should be moved smoothly and in a relaxed way. The circle should be as small as possible in order to make your internally trained force reach the tip of the spear.

ILLUSTRATIONS ON SPEAR PRACTICE FOUND IN THE MILITARY ARTS MANUAL BY CHINESE GENERAL QI JIQUAN (1507–1587) ENTITLED THE *Book of Effective Discipline*.

1a

Asian Martial Arts • Practical Applications 151

## TECHNIQUE 2
### Breeze Shakes Lotus—Circling and Cutting

If your opponent attacks your head with his spear, raise your spear to cross his, and stick and follow his spear. Your body may need to move back slightly **(2a)**. Turn your shaft outward and slightly press down, which should move your opponent's spear off the centerline. Keep sticking to your opponent's spear **(2b)**. Keep your spear in the center and point to his head. Then step forward with your rear foot quickly in order to continue sticking and controlling his spear **(2c)**. If you can get close to your opponent, rotate your spear, and use the tip to attack your opponent **(2d)**. If your opponent moves back, you can step forward to chase and thrust him **(2e)**. Here the key is to use the Taijiquan skills or linking, following, and sticking to control your opponent's spear at all times.

Asian Martial Arts • Practical Applications

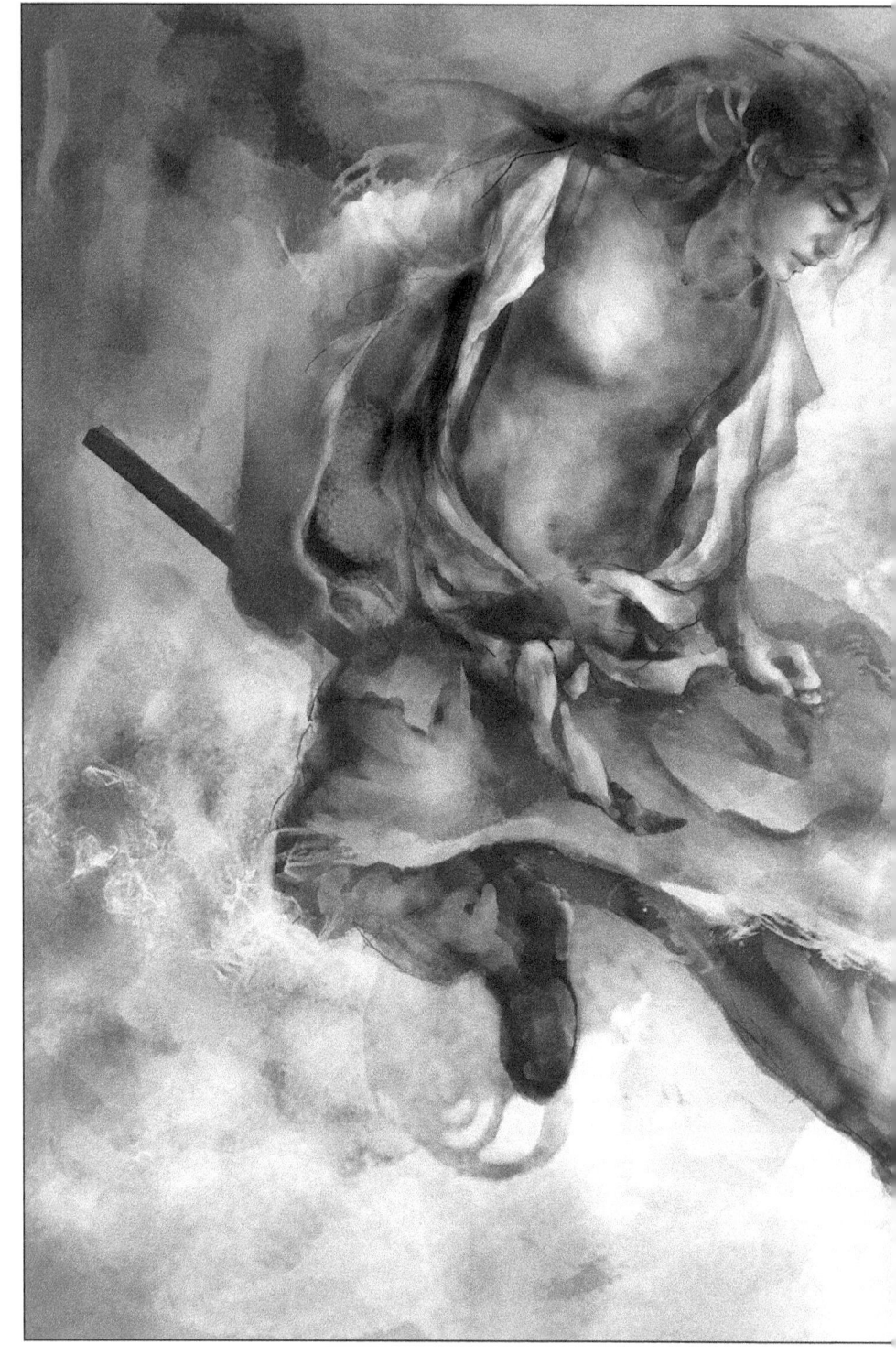

# afterword

"As soon as you have finished a job, you start appreciating the difficulties."

~ Chinese proverb

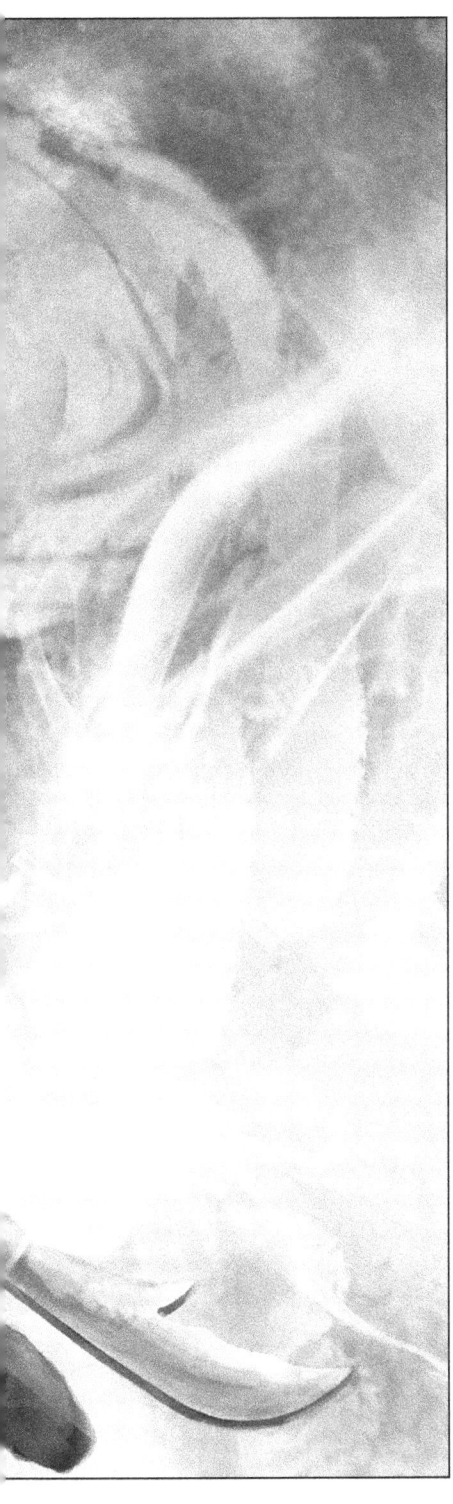

*Illustration by JungShan Inc.*

# The Secrets of an Asian Martial Arts Publisher

Michael A. DeMarco, M.A.

### Tilling the Field of Asian Martial Arts Study

The *Journal of Asian Martial Arts* was founded in 1991 with a long list of objectives for improving the quality of scholarship in this field, as well as raising the standards regarding actual practice. In so many ways, it has failed. As the founder and editor-in-chief of this publication, you may expect that I'd retreat into a corner to mourn, because it is sad that the original objectives were not met. However, if the bar were set low enough, all the goals would have been easily reached. So, rather than mourn, we publish *Asian Martial Arts: Constructive Thoughts and Practical Applications* to celebrate what was accomplished.

I hope this article will be useful to all by illuminating the realities involved in publishing a periodical on this subject. First, we should know the journal's original goals in order to understand its actual accomplishments over two decades. What obstacles blocked the journal's progress and what catalysts helped foster it? At the same time, a close look at these realities helps us understand the evolution of martial arts study and practice over this period, primarily in English-speaking countries.

### Reasons the Journal was Founded

Anyone entering the martial arts for the first time jumps into a flowing stream of cultural influences that contributes to how martial arts are perceived and eventually defined. This vision is highly obscured by bias, fads, salesmanship, Hollywood flair, competitive hype, and a plethora of misinformation. Even if the vision is true according to one perspective, say that of martial sports, it usually neglects the completeness of what martial arts are in their entirety. To a large extent, the view of these combative arts is colored by what is found in print media.

When I started studying a martial art in 1965, judo and karate dominated all media. Karate tournaments grew in popularity. In the U.S., most of the information available came from former military personnel who spent a brief time in Japan, particularly in Okinawa, and had some training. Eventually, and under similar situations, information about martial arts in Korea also started to spread. There was little information about other Asian martial art styles. However, a door was kicked open, and interest in the Asian martial traditions grew.

*Black Belt* magazine (1961) was the first periodical to focus on combatives. Other popular mass-market magazines followed. The movie and television industries also responded to the idea of supply and demand, producing *Kung Fu* (1972–75), *Enter the Dragon* (1973), *The Karate Kid* (1984), and many more movies. Plus, book titles experienced exponential growth. There were some brilliant flashes of insight and substance in these varied forms of media, enmeshed in various degrees of myth, fantasy, fiction, hyperbole, and misinformation. How could anyone discern fact from fiction regarding the true history and culture of Asian combative traditions?

Publications serve as primary reference sources for other media, so it is important to look closely at what was published about martial arts during the 1960s, 1970s, and 1980s. It seems that a large percentage of books and articles dealing with Asian martial traditions lacked true substance. Content was often biased, fueled by ego, or produced for profit and promotion. Texts included many inaccuracies and rarely included any references. Primary sources in Asian languages could be found in a few theses and dissertations, but these were rare occurrences since academia placed little importance on the Asian martial arts as a subject of study. Studies worth mentioning were those scientific articles about martial arts that fell in the areas of health and sports.

Donn Draeger's works stand out in their sincerity and accuracy, derived from solid scholarship and field research. *Asian Fighting Arts* (1969), coauthored with Robert W. Smith, is still in print and used for reference. A number of other books bearing Draeger's name as author also remain strong reference works. By contrast, dozens of books and hundreds of articles were produced by people who lacked qualifications—usually not being familiar with the cultural milieu where the arts developed, often in martial training itself, and sometimes in both of these areas. If a study were done of the published articles and books over these decades, the gems of quality writings would be few and far between.

By 1990, trends in publishing continued, producing more in quantity, but still lacking in quality. A few people tried to raise the standards by publishing periodicals, including *Judo Illustrated* under the hand of Donn Draeger, Hunter Armstrong's *Hoplos*, and Wayne Muromoto's *Fuyru* magazine. All had excellent quality, but were short lived and had limited influence. Plus, the focus remained on the Japanese arts.

While attending college in 1973, I was introduced to Taijiquan by a librarian who also taught Mandarin. He introduced me to a Taiji teacher in Taiwan, and I first traveled there in 1976. My interest in Taiji grew and I tried to collect information from any source. If quality materials dealing with Japanese martial arts were scarce, materials dealing with Chinese arts were more so. Those wishing to gather information about martial traditions from other Asian countries were in a similar predicament. As any serious martial arts practitioner of that time knows, the personal collection of books and articles was inspiring, but not very reliable. And articles in foreign Asian script may have looked important, albeit incomprehensible without the language skills to translate.

I returned to Taiwan in 1984 to study at the National Taiwan Normal University's Mandarin Training Center and continue studies of Taiji. My interests in Chinese culture deepened and I eventually pursued a master's degree from Seton Hall University. This background helped me to look at the martial arts as living traditions that were vital aspects within the cultures where they developed. Sadly, it became more and more apparent how shallow the representation of Asian martial traditions had been in the bulk of mass media. After graduating from the university, I decided to pursue work that I would enjoy and chose to start a serious journal on Asian martial arts. This would combine my academic studies, foreign travel experience, and favorite hobby.

## Setting Goals for the Journal

I enjoyed studying martial arts and also learning about Asian culture. I wanted to go beyond the tournament circuits and *Teenage Mutant Ninja Turtles* (1987). Fiction and fantasy are fine for what they represent, but what was the reality of martial arts practice in Asia? What skills does a true master embody? How and why were the various martial arts developed? There simply was no reliable source that could provide such information. If a journal could be produced, perhaps it would attract qualified writers who would be inspired to contribute by sharing their knowledge and experiences.

The desire to produce a martial arts periodical led to many questions on how to organize it and set editorial goals. The initial vision was simply to provide what had been missing with most publications on the subject: reliable articles about Asian martial traditions. Authors had to be highly skilled in the martial art they wrote about, and preferably had a solid comprehension of the associated culture. The ideal would be to publish articles by knowledgeable, experienced scholar-practitioners. I set out to find people who fit this description. It was like hunting for the elusive unicorn, and some were found!

Standard academic journals served as guides. What were the authors' qualifications? Detailed bios had to be given. Where did the writers get their information? Authors had to provide their references and bibliographies so others could refer to them for reliability. Such guidelines were helpful, but I didn't want to totally limit the journal's readership to a dozen specialists, as many academic journals do. If produced solely for scholars, the articles would not be of much use for the vast majority of readers. It seemed best to keep the writing clear and readable, in plain, college-level English. Writers were asked to put foreign terms in brackets and be sure to provide definitions for any specialized terminology.

For a few millennia, China was a source of inspiration for neighboring peoples. All aspects of Chinese culture, such as medicine, architecture, and arts and crafts, were adapted by these bordering states. The martial arts were not an exception, and the Chinese influence can easily be seen in nearby Korea, Japan, and Southeast Asia, for example. Because of China's profound influence, it was natural that Chinese martial traditions should be included in every journal.

Japanese martial arts were popular, plus they have a wonderful tradition of preservation through unbroken lines of instruction and solid historic documentation. We decided each journal should include at least one article about Japan.

What of the other areas and their unique martial art heritage? Kalaripayattu. Bando. Silat. … Hundreds of styles had names that were not yet well known in the West. Few could write about these rare styles. Some who pioneered studies in these lesser-known areas were born in European countries that had established long political relationships in Asia. For example, the Dutch wrote about the indigenous fighting arts of Indonesia, the French about Vietnamese fighting arts, and the British about Indian arts. Obtaining new articles on these lesser-known arts was difficult.

The search for qualified authors included writing letters to scholarly and martial art organizations, as well as to individual scholars and practitioners. A number of references were utilized, such as directories for Asian specialists and martial artists. From those contacted, some responded to the solicitation for articles.

The journal's title was selected and submissions were received. What next? Scholars from various areas of specialization were invited to participate with work on the journal and an editorial board was formed. Members would be helpful to review submissions, fact-check, edit, proof, and hopefully help bring in article submissions due to their professional contacts. Editorial guidelines were developed.

Next came the actual design of the physical journal: page size, type, layouts, logo, etc. Finding a printer was easy enough. Materials also had to be submitted to distributors with hopes to get journals into bookstores. We eventually worked with more than a dozen distributors that delivered the journal to all the major bookstore chains and many independent bookstores throughout the U.S. and Canada, plus some distribution to other foreign countries in Europe and Asia. The graphic elements from the journal design facilitated designing our first website.

**Starting Via Media Publishing Company**

All the plans to start the physical journal were made, but an actual business also needed to be legally founded. How to do this without much experience in publishing, and without financial backing? A company name was chosen in order to produce the periodical: Via Media Publishing. The name has overtones of Asian philosophy, since via means "way, path, or road," and media is the "middle" or what comes in between. A cost-effective location was soon found: my parents' attic!

Via Media Publishing Company was embedded in the family home. The attic was the main office, with file cabinets, typewriter, and a newfangled thing called a computer—my first Macintosh, with which I could magically "cut and paste." The kitchen table served as the place to take phone orders, equipped with a charge card machine and record books. The dining room and living room became the shipping department for mailings every three months when a new journal was printed. Journals were stored in the basement and boxed or placed in padded mailers for any orders that came in between bulk mailings. Via Media didn't have digital products: the internet was starting to expand, but wasn't commercialized until 1995.

We prepared the house for work and prepared computer files and artwork for press. What were needed were orders. Over twenty thousand tri-fold announcements were mailed to martial art schools, libraries, and academic departments associated with Asian studies. The flyer included a postcard with the journal logo, details about the journal, and ordering information. I told my mom that perhaps we should put a big cardboard box under the regular mailbox to handle the response from the mass mailing. We waited daily in anticipation, but found we never needed an extra box.

## Realities of Publishing the *Journal of Asian Martial Arts*

Our goal was to publish a serious periodical about Asian martial arts according to scholarly standards. This had never been successfully done before. After all was set in motion for publishing—journal design, article submissions, editing, printing, distribution, business organization—how would the journal be accepted?

When the journal was first announced in 1992, regular practitioners thought it sounded too scholarly and weren't interested. Academicians thought the subject not worthy to consider reading or including in a library. Whenever practitioners did see an issue, they found that it included techniques they could learn. When academics somehow opened the pages, they were surprised to see the scholarly articles were of high standard. The journal mixed heavier academic pieces with others of lighter reading. The number of subscribers slowly grew.

Scholarly tools are necessary in order to accurately present the martial arts. Each area of academic specialization can contribute to a clearer picture and understanding of this subject. We welcomed approaches from all academic disciplines: anthropology, history, linguistics, economics, philosophy, literature, law, physical education, sociology, etc. However, academic studies alone cannot fully present all aspects of the combative arts. Martial art masters were often illiterate, which does not detract from their great skills and insights. Reports, interviews, reflections, and "how to" articles are vital for understanding combat traditions. There were hundreds of article submissions, and each was considered for publication on its own merits.

We hoped that the quality and quantity of article submissions would improve with time by attracting writers who wanted to help improve the field with their experience and knowledge. Articles could inspire others to expand upon published pieces, follow up with further research, and bring new knowledge and insights to readers. People could collaborate, bringing individual talents and skills together to offer what no one single author could do alone.

As work began on each upcoming issue, we always worried that there would not be enough good material to fill it. As mentioned, most articles were rejected due to poor writing and research. It is easy to tell when an article is submitted as a promotion piece, an attempt to sell a product or service. A good number of academic-style articles looked scholarly, but didn't possess content worth publishing. Some scholarly articles were excellent, but only a few people could comprehend or benefit from the presentations. The long-joked-about formula "KISS: keep it simple, scholar," is unfortunately ignored by most who need to think about the real purpose of writing. Who are they writing for? Sometimes the more educated people become, the more they equate the use of foreign terms, specialized vocabulary, and complex sentence structure as their claim for being an authority. Ironically, many highly educated scholars were not smart enough to know how to write clearly for those outside their clique.

Dress like a samurai and you can take on the aura. Does writing with a mix of Japanese and English make one sound more educated? Some writers insisted on using Japanese terms according to Japanese usage. For example, "I practice *kata*." Is kata here singular or plural? In Japanese it is both, but not in English. Our journal is in English. The word *kata* has been absorbed into English and the plural is *katas*. However, to a westerner who has spent years trying to live and speak as a Japanese, it just doesn't seem right using "katas" in an English sentence.

The journal also utilized pinyin romanization from Chinese. Accordingly, we would use *Daoism*, *Xingyi*, and *Taijiquan* rather than *Taoism*, *Hsing-i*, or *T'ai Chi Ch'uan*. The journal utilized such styles for academic reasons, not because of some whim, personal preference, or habit. Many potential authors could not adapt.

One writer submitted an excellent, well-written article. The ideas were insightful and would have benefited many readers. For such important articles, we required that sources be given so readers would know where the author obtained the information and could also follow up if they wished. All authors rehash old material. Better authors learn from others' writings and experiences, analyze them, and build upon them. In this case, when I asked the author to provide sources—books, articles, personal communications, etc.—he simply replied: "But Mike, I am the authority!" Sorry, this isn't good enough. This guy may be an authority, but only because he built upon others' work.

When we published the article "People and Events of Taekwondo's Formative Years," by Dakin Burdick (Volume 6 Number 1, 1996: 30–49), a number of people who practiced Taekwondo were outraged. The article showed that this art actually was derived from Japanese styles, debunking the belief that the style was purely Korean. A famous instructor in the U.S. sent a facsimile to me stating, "Taekwondo is Korean." No proof. No references. Just his brief statement. Why should anyone believe him?

Another famous teacher submitted an article about Taiji for publication. I had some drawings made for the front of the article. After she saw the publication, she was furious. "That illustration looks like a man!" she said. I thought, "Well, Ms. Prima Donna, it wasn't supposed to be you." She threatened me with a lawsuit. So much for the peaceful ways of Taiji and character building.

There were other articles submitted by well-known practitioners. Some articles were written well enough, but they didn't offer anything new. A few authors wrote about their masters, how they became disciples, and how they inherited the system, but didn't provide any new insights or information for our readers. I wanted material that had not been published elsewhere, and that would at least offer something fresh.

If any submission had potential, I would offer some feedback and suggestions. This is the work of an editor-in-chief. When authors were willing to work together, the end result would be an improved article that exceeded the author's original quest in quality. Others were offended that anyone could make any suggestions at all. They were deities above questioning. A number of times I was physically challenged to fisticuffs for offering suggestions or rejecting articles. Threats rather than cooperation. Their martial art skills may have been tops, but their character left much to be desired. Perhaps something missing in their training in the dojo, or even in the nursery school sandbox?

For twenty years we worried about having enough quality material for each issue. It would have been great to have enough material for two issues, so we could get ahead of schedule. That never happened.

Besides constantly worrying about article submissions, publishing requires much time to deal with production, distribution, advertising/promotion, orders, fulfillment, and to handle communications with subscribers. At one time we had a professional company handle advertising for the journal. Their work involved finding companies to purchase advertising space, receiving payments, and paying us after subtracting fees for their services. But they kept all the income! Clear robbery. Lawyers didn't want to pursue collection because there was not enough money in it for them. I eventually found one who would do it for the principal, won, and got paid. Others failed to pay for invoices, including advertisers, bookstores, distributors, and individuals.

Distributors paid whatever they wished. There was no way to know exactly how many journals sold through stores. Income varied greatly each quarter. As the world economy started to weaken, sometimes no payments were received from distributors. They paid bigger publishers, not smaller ones. Eventually, many distributors went bankrupt. Bookstores closed, including the Borders chain. In the end, many payments due Via Media remain unpaid.

Perhaps the biggest problem for us involved website design and maintenance, necessary for customer relations and providing products. Thousands of dollars were spent for promised services, especially in preparation for entering the digital age. Unfortunately, one company after another failed to provide the services agreed upon. So, the website always had problems. It was not user-friendly. Customers got frustrated, so many stopped trying to order products. Can't blame them.

During recent years there has been a decline in the quality of services proved in printing, distribution, fulfillment, and with website work. Costs are all increasing for less services. At the same time all costs were going up, our income decreased. In hard times, conventional wisdom says you stop any periodical subscriptions. Journal subscriptions slowed as expected. All other companies dealing with martial arts suffered as well. Enrollment in all martial art schools dwindled, and thousands of schools closed. Companies supplying products to these schools were forced into bankruptcy, to close, or at minimum to cut back. As part of the supply line, these companies could not afford to purchase advertising. Even the largest companies started to penny pinch.

I thought, maybe the economy will turn around. Maybe martial artists will want to delve deeper into the arts they practice. Leading martial arts scholars and practitioners will surely desire to help the journal improve by offering their input and quality articles. Now I think not in my lifetime. Twenty years of devotion to this field is enough, so we turn the last journal page. Others can carry on from here. Maybe I'll go sip tea in a bamboo grove.

**Publishing Pleasures**

As you can see from the preceding pages, there were many obstacles in publishing the journal. The fact that it was produced for twenty years indicates that there was some support: dedicated subscribers who never missed an issue, authors with a passion for research and commitment to enrich the field, long-time practitioners who generously shared their insights, and associate editors who helped polish articles into smooth reading. Unfortunately, the support was not enough to hold up a serious martial arts publication.

Beside the published articles, there is not much to show. No edifice for Via Media Publishing. No big list of awards or recognitions. However, it seems there were two great benefits. One is that producing the journal has been educational, covering all aspects of publishing, and primarily as an unique way to learn about martial traditions and their place in world history. The second and more important benefit is that this business served as a foyer where many strangers met, drawn by a common interest. Some became comrades in martial studies, and a smaller group became friends.

I have many memories of working with Robert W. Smith on Via Media's first book project: *Martial Musings: A Portrayal of Martial Arts in the 20th Century*. We had many conversations about martial arts and the colorful array of characters in this field, especially the self-proclaimed "masters." Smith's share of bitter experiences brought out his great wit and humor. He valued family over anything involving combatives, and that is a rare trait among martial art addicts.

I've also been blessed to personally meet with another luminary in this field, the late Oscar Ratti, a pioneer known for books he coauthored with his wife, Adele Westbrook. Oscar was not only the consummate martial scholar-practitioner, but a living renaissance man. His grasp of martial traditions, Eastern and Western, was extraordinary. His comprehension of martial traditions was thorough in both theory and application. He was so far ahead of his time that few could carry on a dialogue with him. The self-appointed leaders of martial studies were still doing basic addition and subtraction while Oscar was doing calculus. Physically formidable, this consistently polite man preferred seclusion to limelight. Despite being such a brilliant person, Oscar had a humble heart of gold that was filled with compassion for humankind. He didn't carry any of his great accomplishments on his sleeve, nor did he brag by waving the flag of ego. Signore Ratti was a rare gem in the martial arts world, and it was an honor to know him as a friend.

This book you hold now is also a result of friendships built during the double-decade life of the *Journal of Asian Martial Arts*. Everyone who participated in this production did so out of friendship and a dedication to the spirit of the journal. These brothers- and sisters-in-arms answered a call without hesitation, all agreeing immediately to contribute. I admire all for their academic astuteness in this area of study and for their mastery of combative skills. In addition, I feel they represent a great group of respectful characters!

## Finale

With a few paragraphs, we conclude this book and a celebration in tribute to the *Journal of Asian Martial Arts*. Both the successes and failures of the journal affected many involved in combative arts. If looked at closely, this publishing experience offers insights into the present state of Asian martial arts research and practice, and can benefit future endeavors in this field.

The original vision for the journal naively set goals that were impossible to achieve. That's clear to state now, but it wasn't two decades ago. We simply gave it our best effort and progress was made. The journal set an example for how academic tools could be applied in the field, such as incorporating standards in objectivity, linguistics, and referencing. As a result, there is certainly a stronger drive today to utilize a scholarly approach in writings dealing with martial traditions. In response, other periodical and book publishers raised their standards.

Rather than feature "how to" punch and kick articles, we strived to provide an editorial mix that enriched the combative side of Asian culture. Whenever you deal with true fighting arts, aspects of religion and medicine are naturally affiliated. Among any thinking hominids, ethical questions arise, including who should be taught lethal arts, and what are the responsibilities of both teachers and students. Without reflection and self-cultivation, we are doomed to suffer the consequences of failing to consider the seriousness of combatives as a part of the culture in which we live. Leaders in this field have a responsibility for the role martial art activities play in society, particularly as seen in acts of violence.

As vital cultural threads, the various martial arts have added color to every individual Asian milieu. Plus, like wet ink, they have stained others through cultural contacts. We are fortunate today that a number of fine scholars from all academic disciplines are applying their expertise to the study of martial traditions. The journal has introduced many of these scholars to its readers through their articles. Journal work has also introduced some scholars to each other, stimulating individual and collaborative efforts found in other publications and film documentaries.

Considering the journal's accomplishments as presented above, we know that they are just baby steps in the long trek toward what can still be accomplished in this field. For example, linguists should offer standard guidelines for romanization and provide clear definitions for related terminology. Weaponry and martial systems could be classified according to time and place. Writers can build upon previously published journal articles, verifying, expanding, and filling in missing areas of research.

Perhaps the most important part of martial arts scholarly research lies not in academia itself, but in the actual practice of these arts today and in the future. Why should people practice these arts in the first place? The answer will certainly include aspects of self-defense, law enforcement, artistic expression, sport, physical exercise, and therapy. Some instructors say they teach for health, but they often lack knowledge in basic human anatomy and kinetics. Many teach for self-defense, but their techniques may prove useless on the street. Olympic trainers focus on developing athletes, and often fail to incorporate new scientific studies to help their students. All of these martially-inspired expressions can benefit from scholarly studies, and hint at the enormous work that awaits for the serious scholar-practitioner.

Illustration by JungShan Inc.

Sorry to admit, but progress in this field will continue to be hindered by apathy, superficiality, super egos, jealousy, and uncooperativeness. I've been surprised that, after twenty years, the journal's main goals were not even understood by most associate editors! I hope that others more capable than I will be able to make solid advances in this field. Universities could support a martial arts publication, as does the University of Leon in Spain (www.revistadeartesmarciales.com). Scholarly conferences can either include panels on Asian martial arts, or be the sole focus for conferences. Books and articles by qualified individuals and coauthors will no doubt continue to be a growing influence.

What influence will martial arts play in our future? Some say they have no interest in the martial arts because combatives are strongly associated with violence. True, but although we do not like cancer, we certainly hope that some are studying it seriously. Likewise for the martial traditions, which are vital, evolving aspects of our human cultural tapestry. As such, we should not let the fighting arts spread haphazardly under the whims of ego, profit, and the primal release of violent instincts.

Unlike most physical activities, especially those associated with sports and recreation, the martial arts stand out for their potential to harm, maim, and kill. Just how these arts develop in the following decades will be determined by those having the most influence in sociopolitical affairs. Will they fail to take these arts seriously, as they have done with other cultural elements? Or will they become more responsible in handling this double-edged sword?

I now bow out with sincere thanks to all who have supported the *Journal of Asian Martial Arts* by subscribing, submitting articles, and advertising. Hopefully it has inspired your study and practice over the decades. May all continue to safely enjoy and benefit from your responsible involvement in the Asian martial traditions.

## materials for research and practice • books

- **Advancing in Taekwondo 2nd Ed.**
  Author: Grandmaster Richard Chun. Description: Originally published in 1983, this authoritative work has been the guide for thousands of Taekwondo Black Belts as they advanced in their training. Publisher: YMAA Publication Center, Inc.
  ‣ www.ymaa.com/publishing

- **Aikido Exercises for Teaching and Training**
  Author: C. M. Shifflett. Description: An ideal companion for Aikido teachers and students of all systems, this book offers over 100 illustrations and 300 pages of detailed techniques and exercises. ‣ www.bluesnakebooks.com

- **Aikido: My Spiritual Journey**
  Authors: Gozo Shioda; Yasuhisa Shioda (Afterword). Description: Grandmaster Shioda tells of his training under Morihei Ueshiba, his founding of the Yoshinkan Aikido, and his work with the Tokyo police department and several universities. Publisher: Kodansha USA. ‣ www.kodanshausa.com

- **The Art of Chinese Swordsmanship: A Manual of Taiji Jian**
  Author: Yun Zhang. Description: English-language introduction to the Taiji sword. Includes history, fundamental principles, and essential thirty-two postures. Publisher: Blue Snake Books. ‣ www.bluesnakebooks.com

- **The Art of Japanese Swordsmanship: A Manual of Eishin Ryu Iaido**
  Author: Nicklaus Suino. Description: This manual is illustrated with step-by-step drawings to help all students hone their forms and techniques. Publisher: Weatherhill. ‣ www.shambhala.com

- **Bagua Linked Palms / Swimming Body Palms**
  Author: Wang Shujin; Kent Howard and Chen Hsiao-Yen, Trans. Description: This book offers a grounding in the basics of Bagua principles and practice from a renowned Bagua Zhang expert. ‣ www.bluesnakebooks.com

- **Best Karate, Volumes 1 through 11**
  Author: Masatoshi Nakayama. Description: All the karate and kumite practiced by the Japan Karate Association. Each volume includes drawings, diagrams, and numerous photos of an instructor demonstrating the techniques. Publisher: Kodansha USA. ‣ www.kodanshausa.com

- **Budo Mind and Body: Training Secrets of the Japanese Martial Arts**
  Author: Nicklaus Suino. Description: Advice on how to get the most from training in traditional Japanese martial arts such as iaido, kendo, aikido, judo, and karate-do. Publisher: Weatherhill. ‣ http://artofjapaneseswordsmanship.com

- **The Character of Goju-Ryu: Kata Implications for Experienced Practitioners**

Author: Rich Stamper. Description: Interpretation and understanding using kata as textbooks. Differentiates traditional from classical practice. Goju-Ryu specific but applicable to all styles. Assumes kata competence. Photographs, 393 pages. Publisher: GKK Publications. ‣ www.goju.com

- *Chen Style Taijiquan: The Source of Taiji Boxing*
  Authors: David Gaffney and Davidine Siaw-Voon Sim. Description: Introduction to Chen-style taijiquan history and legends, outlines the major forms, discusses the philosophy and foundation of the art, and also covers training methods, push hands, and weapons. Publisher: North Atlantic Books. ‣ www.amazon.com

- *Chinese Martial Arts Cinema: The Wuxia Tradition*
  Author: Stephen Teo. Description: Unveils the rich layers of the wuxia tradition as it developed in 1920s Shanghai, and from the 1950s in Hong Kong and Taiwan. Publisher: Edinburgh University Press.
  ‣ www.euppublishing.com/book/9780748632862

- *Die Chinesische Kampfkunst: Spiegel und Element Traditioneller Chinesischer Kultur* (*Chinese Fighting Arts: Mirror and Element of Traditional Chinese Culture*)
  Author: Kai Filipiak. Description: Scholarly coverage of Chinese martial arts by this associate professor of Chinese studies at Leipzig University. Publisher: Leipzig Univeristy Press. ‣ www.amazon.de

- *Chojun—a novel*
  Author: Goran Powell. Description: Two lives joined in karate, an island torn apart by war. Reverence, coming of age, love, tragedy, war, and honor come together in this gripping historical fiction about the man who is undeniably one of the most influential karate masters of the twentieth century. Publisher: YMAA Publication Center, Inc. ‣ www.ymaa.com/publishing

- *Combat Techniques of Taiji, Xingyi, and Bagua*
  Author: Lu Shengli; Yun Zhang, Trans. Description: Selects core movements from Taiji, Bagua, and Xingyi as taught by Wang Peisheng. Allows one to recognize the unique strategies and skills, and to develop a deeper understanding of each style. Publisher: Blue Snake Books. ‣ www.bluesnakebooks.com

- *Complete Kendo*
  Author: John Donohue. Description: A thorough introduction to the Japanese martial way of the sword, *Complete Kendo* covers every aspect of the discipline, from equipment and terminology to technique and strategy. Also provides a solid overview of the art's principles and philosophy. Photos throughout. Publisher: Tuttle Publishing. ‣ www.tuttlepublishing.com

- *The Complete Taiji Dao: The Art of the Chinese Saber*
  Author: Yun Zhang. Description: Broad in scope and detailed in its presentation of the principles and practice of Taiji dao. Also provides illustrated discussions of the history of Chinese swords. Publisher: Blue Snake Books. ‣ www.bluesnakebooks.com
- *The Cutting Season—A Xenon Pearl Martial Arts Thriller*
  Author: Arthur Rosenfeld. Description: In this life, Dr. Xenon Pearl must use his skill to defend the innocent, defeat the Russian mob, protect the woman who loves him, and stay one step ahead of a smart cop; he is set to lose everything unless he can cut just one more time. Publisher: YMAA Publication Center, Inc. ‣ www.ymaa.com/publishing
- *Deshi: A Martial Arts Thriller*
  Author: John Donohue. Description: Connor Burke labors as a *deshi*, a student under the tutelage of a master warrior—a practice that draws him into the execution-style murder of a Japanese businessman, into the dangers of a lethal samurai heritage, and finally, into the unknown darkness of an elite mountain temple where Connor's deadliest challenge awaits. Publisher: Onyx. ‣ www.amazon.com
- *Dukkha—The Suffering, A Sam Reeve Martial Arts Thriller*
  Author: Loren W. Christensen. Description: In the course of a single week, everything Sam Reeves believed in, everything he knew, everyone he trusted, all would be put on the line for a family he never knew he had. This high-octane martial arts thriller will have you gripped from the start. Publisher: YMAA Publication Center, Inc. ‣ www.ymaa.com/publishing
- *The Eight Immortals' Revolving Sword*
  Author: Wu Baolin, McBride, M. and Wu, V. Description: Details the esoteric sword practice Dr. Wu learned at the White Cloud Monastery in Beijing. Explains its history, theory, cosmology, and practice in great detail. Publisher: Three Pines Press. ‣ www.lulu.com
- *Encyclopedia of Japanese Martial Arts*
  Author: David A. Hall. Description: Authoritative and comprehensive, this invaluable reference work by a leading authority on Japanese martial arts provides clear, reliable information on every aspect of the subject. Publisher: Kodansha USA. ‣ www.kodanshausa.com
- *The Essence of Budo: A Practitioner's Guide to Understanding the Japanese Martial Ways*
  Author: David Lowry. Description: The study of *budo*, or Japanese martial arts, for self-cultivation is a lifelong path toward achieving perfect balance in body, mind, and spirit. Lowry addresses the myriad issues, vagaries, and inconsistencies that arise for students of Japanese martial arts—classical and modern—as their training develops. Publisher: Shambhala Publications. ‣ www.shambhala.com

- *The Essence of Budo: The Secret Teachings of the Grandmaster*
  Author: Masaaki Hatsumi. Description: Hatsumi offers insights into the spiritual path that all martial artists must take, reveals secret techniques and hidden principles, and elucidates the words of his master, Toshitsugu Takamatsu. Publisher: Kodansha USA. ‣ www.kodanshausa.com
- *The Essence of Karate*
  Authors: Gichin Funakoshi, Hirokazu Kanazawa (Foreword), Gisho Funakoshi (Afterword). Description: Philosophical and anecdotal writings from the father of modern karate explore the essence and history of the martial art, and recall his own training and work. Publisher: Kodansha USA. ‣ www.kodanshausa.com
- *The Essence of Shaolin White Crane—Martial Power and Qigong*
  Author: Dr. Yang, Jwing-Ming. Description: Internal power is revealed in this expert guide to internal and external martial qigong. Martial arts qigong is integral to White Crane Kung Fu and is a proven way to build explosive fighting power, known as *Jin*. Publisher: YMAA Publication Center, Inc. ‣ www.ymaa.com/publishing
- *The Essence of Taijiquan*
  Authors: David Gaffney and Davidine Siaw-Voon Sim. Description: Endorsed by Grandmaster Chen Xiaowang. A comprehensive look at some of the deeper aspects of Chen Taijiquan. Includes insights from some of today's leading practitioners. Publisher: CTGB-Blurb. ‣ www.blurb.com
- *Herding the Ox: The Martial Arts as Moral Metaphor*
  Author: John Donohue. Description: This book uses Zen-inspired illustrations as a springboard to discuss the spiritual and ethical dimensions of martial arts training. Publisher: Turtle Press. ‣ www.turtlepress.com
- *Hidden Hands: Unlocking the Secrets of Traditional Martial Arts Forms*
  Author: Phillip Starr. Description: Containing examples from Chinese, Japanese, Okinawan, and Korean martial arts, *Hidden Hands* shows serious practitioners how to improve in any art and style. Publisher: Blue Snake Books. ‣ www.bluesnakebooks.com
- *In the Dojo: A Guide to the Rituals and Etiquette of the Japanese Martial Arts*
  Author: David Lowry. Description: This book illuminates the history and meaning behind the rituals, training costumes, objects, and relationships that have such profound significance in Japanese martial arts. Publisher: Weatherhill. ‣ www.shambhala.com
- *Iron Shirt Chi Kung*
  Author: Mantak Chia. Description: An introduction to this ancient practice that describes the unique Iron Shirt air-packing techniques that protect vital organs from injuries, establishes roots to the earth's energy, and unifies physical, mental, and spiritual health. Publisher: Inner Traditions.
  ‣ Website: http://store.innertraditions.com/isbn/978-1-59477-104-0

- *Jet Li: Chinese Masculinity and Transnational Film Stardom*
  Author: Sabrina Qiong Yu. Description: Yu uses Li as an example to address some intriguing but under-examined issues surrounding transnational stardom in general and transnational kung fu stardom in particular. Publisher: Edinburgh University Press. ‣ www.euppublishing.com/book/9780748645473
- *Jingwu: The School that Transformed Kung Fu*
  Authors: Brian Kennedy and Elizabeth Guo. Description: This lively history tells the story of the seminal Jingwu Association, founded to keep Chinese martial arts traditions alive in the face of modern weaponry. Publisher: Blue Snake Books.
  ‣ www.bluesnakebooks.com
- *Kage: The Shadow: A Connor Burke Martial Arts Thriller*
  Author: John Donohue. Description: *Kage* builds on the characters and plots of the previous Burke novels *Sensei, Deshi,* and *Tengu*. It advances the ever-deepening relationship between student and teacher while weaving in time-honored themes of the martial arts: conduct, ordeal, and courage, with events as current as today's headlines. Publisher: YMAA Publication Center, Inc. ‣ www.ymaa.com/publishing
- *Karate: A Master's Secrets of Uechi-Ryu*
  Author: Ihor Rymaruk. Description: Reviews: "This book may be the most useful and practical book on Uechi-Ryu." "It offers invaluable insight into the discipline and will no doubt become a historical landmark." Publisher: Iron Arm International. ‣ www.UechiRyu-karate.com
- *Karate Kenpo: The Art of Self-defense*
  Author: Mabuni Kenwa; Mario McKenna, Trans. Description: Introduces Mabuni Kenwa's ideas about the history and development of karatedo on Okinawa, warm-ups, basic techniques, stances, training equipment, and the katas Sanchin and Seiunchin. Press: Lulu Press. ‣ www.lulu.com/spotlight/bechurinatgmail.com
- *The Karate Way: Discovering the Spirit of Practice*
  Author: David Lowry. Description: The author illuminates the complete path of karate, including practice, philosophy, and culture. He covers myriad subjects of interest to karate practitioners of all ages and levels. Publisher: Shambhala Publications. ‣ www.shambhala.com
- *Kodokan Judo*
  Author: Jigoro Kano. Description: The most authoritative guide to Kodokan judo by its creator covers everything from fundamental concepts and techniques to formal exercises. Fully illustrated throughout. Publisher: Kodansha USA.
  ‣ www.kodanshausa.com
- *Kurikara: The Sword and the Serpent*
  Author: John Maki Evans, Foreword by Natanaga Zhander. Description: The first

foreign student to Nakamura Taisaburo sensei, John Maki Evans lays out the eight basic principles of swordsmanship common to all Japanese sword schools. Publisher: Blue Snake Books. ‣ www.bluesnakebooks.com

- **Martial Musings: A Portrayal of Martial Arts in the 20th Century**
  Author: Robert W. Smith. Description: This book stands out as the sole literary work that offers readers a unique perspective of martial arts as they evolved during the twentieth century. By a pioneer in martial arts research in America. Publisher: Via Media Publishing. ‣ www.journalofasianmartialarts.com

- **Meditations on Violence: A Comparison of Martial Arts Training and Real World Violence**
  Author: Sgt. Rory Miller. Description: Experienced martial artist and veteran correction officer Sgt. Rory Miller distills what he has learned from jailhouse brawls, tactical operations, and ambushes to explore the differences between martial arts and the subject martial arts were designed to deal with: violence. Publisher: YMAA Publication Center, Inc. ‣ www.ymaa.com/publishing

- **Old Frame Chen Family Taijiquan**
  Author: Mark Chen. Description: History, principles, and explanation of the old Chen style of taijiquan, with pictorial descriptions of the first form, basic postures, and push-hands exercises. Publisher: Blue Snake Books. ‣ www.northatlanticbooks.com

- **An Overview of Karatedo**
  Author: Nakasone Genwa (Ed.); Mario McKenna, Trans. Description: One of the most comprehensive books published during the golden age of karatedo containing chapters by Shiroma Shimpan, Hanashiro Chomo, Mabuni Kenwa, Otsuka Hironori, and Taira Shinken. Press: Lulu Press.
  ‣ www.lulu.com/spotlight/bechurinatgmail.com

- **Persimmon Wind: A Martial Artist's Journey in Japan**
  Author: David Lowry. Description: Part memoir, martial arts history, and part travelogue, Dave Lowry relates experiences as he travels to Japan to explore a country and culture that profoundly influenced his life. Publisher: Koryu Books. ‣ www.koryu.com

- **The Power of Internal Martial Arts and Chi: Combat and Energy Secrets of Ba Gua, Tai Chi and Hsing-I**
  Author: Bruce Frantzis. Description: This classic book examines the three main internal martial arts—tai chi (taiji), hsing-i (xingyi), and ba gua (pakua)—and their substyles. ‣ www.bluesnakebooks.com

- **Practice Drills for Japanese Swordsmanship**
  Author: Nicklaus Suino. Description: Enhances training by providing wooden-sword drills to supplement the formal class activity of forms practice. Publisher: Weatherhill. ‣ www.shambhala.com

- *Ryukyu Kobudo: The Students of Taira Shinken*
  Author: Mario McKenna. Description: Presents an overview of the life of Taira Shinken, his students, and the weapons tradition he passed on. Includes detailed photos and notes on the Ryukyu Kobudo kata. Press: Lulu Press.
  ‣ www.lulu.com/spotlight/bechurinatgmail.com
- *The Samurai Sword: Introduction and Application*
  Author: Dana Gregory Abbott. Description: This book's purpose and intent focus on "How To" wield a Japanese sword in a strong, direct, practical manner while answering all your questions. Publisher: Amethyst Moon.
  ‣ www.streetsmartsamurai.com
- *Scientific Coaching for Olympic Taekwondo*
  Authors: Willy Pieter and John Heijmans. Description: This is the first book on coaching Taekwondo based on scientific research. Chapters include information on periodization, endurance, strength, psychological profiles, and injuries. Publisher: Meyer and Meyer Sport. ‣ www.amazon.com
- *Sensei*
  Author: John Donohue. Description: A modern-day masterless samurai is traveling across the country, systematically murdering martial arts masters. Publisher: Onyx.
  ‣ www.amazon.com
- *Shin Gi Tai: Karate Training for Body, Mind, and Spirit*
  Author: Michael Clarke. Description: Within these pages, you will discover traditional karate; along the way, perhaps many of your own beliefs about karate will be confronted. You might have a body capable of mastering karate's physical techniques, but do you have a mind with a level of awareness that is able to grasp the true spirit of karate? Publisher: YMAA Publication Center, Inc.
  ‣ www.ymaa.com/publishing
- *Shaolin Qi Gong*
  Author: Shi Xinggui. Description: Authentic qi gong as practiced in the Shaolin Temple, where this discipline originated centuries ago. Book includes a 53-minute DVD of exercises performed by the author, a Shaolin monk. Publisher: Inner Traditions. ‣ http://store.innertraditions.com/isbn/978-1-59477-264-1
- *Sinmoo Hapkido Curriculum Handbook*
  Author: Sean Bradley. Description: Complete curriculum handbook (white belt to fourth degree) for Sinmoo Hapkido as taught by its founder, Dojunim Ji Han-Jae. Publisher: Sean Bradley. ‣ www.lulu.com
- *The Spirit of Aikido*
  Authors: Kisshomaru Ueshiba, Moriteru Ueshiba (Preface). Description: Now available in hardcover as well as the popular paperback edition, Kisshomaru

Ueshiba's masterwork explains the essence of the techniques of aikido. New photos and preface. Publisher: Kodansha USA. ▸ www.kodanshausa.com

- **Strategy in Japanese Swordsmanship**
  Author: Nicklaus Suino. Description: A framework for learning strategy in swordsmanship, along with techniques and drills that help put the strategies into practice. Publisher: Weatherhill. ▸ www.shambhala.com

- **The Study of Seipai: The Secrets of Self-defense Karate Kenpo**
  Author: Mabuni Kenwa; Mario McKenna, Trans. Description: The second written works of Mabuni Kenwa focusing on the performance and applications of the kata Seipai. Press: Lulu Press. ▸ www.lulu.com/spotlight/bechurinatgmail.com

- **Tai Chi in Your Life**
  Author: Dale Napier. Description: A discussion of eight major Tai Chi principles: How to apply them to your everyday life, using examples from martial arts and from life. Publisher: MasterSoft. ▸ www.TaiChiInYourLife.com

- **Tales of the Hermit, Vols. I, II, and III** Graphic novel series.
  Authors: O. Ratti and A. Westbrook. Description: "This large-sized volume, filled with telling drawings and incisive scenes of mortal combat, is a brilliantly rendered spiritual lesson, stunningly original and exquisitely imaginative." ~ *The Book Reader*. Publisher: Via Media Publishing. ▸ www.journalofasianmartialarts.com

- **The Teachings of Karatedô**
  Author: Heiko Bittmann. Description: Based on a doctoral dissertation, this book presents rare English translations of karatedô texts with explanations. In some cases, these are the only English translations. Extensive bibliography. Publisher: Verlag Heiko Bittmann. ▸ www.bittmann-verlag.com

- **Tengu the Mountain Goblin: A Connor Burke Martial Arts Thriller**
  Author: John Donohue. Description: A renegade martial arts sensei known as the Tengu has been recruited to train a splinter group of Asian terrorists with links to Al Qaeda. Publisher: YMAA Publications. ▸ http://ymaa.com/publishing

- **Theater & Martial Arts in West Sumatra: Randai & Silek of the Minangkabau**
  Author: Kirstin Pauka. Description: The strong presence of the indigenous martial arts (*silek*) is illustrated in the focus of the stories that are told through *randai*, a popular folk theater tradition. Publisher: Ohio University Press. ▸ www.ohioswallow.com

- **Traditional Taekwondo: Core Techniques, History, and Philosophy**
  Author: Doug Cook. Description: History and evolution of Taekwondo from its ancient roots to modern-day applications. Includes exercises for internal energy development, meditation, and practical self-defense strategies. Focuses on the traditional aspects of Taekwondo rather than on its sportive component. Publisher: YMAA Publication Center, Inc. ▸ www.ymaa.com/publishing

- *Traditions: Essays on the Japanese Martial Arts and Ways*
  Author: David Lowry. Description: This collection of essays discusses the techniques, methods, and rituals of Japanese martial art masters, which also serve as guides to a well-lived life. Publisher: Tuttle Publishing.
  › www.tuttlepublishing.com
- **Tai Chi for Kids**
  Authors: Jose Figueroa and Stephan Berwick Description: Unique for kids! Presenting a game-playing approach, the publication offers unique teaching and practice methods derived from one of the author's successful experience teaching Chen Taiji to public school children. www.truetaichi.com
- **Taijiquan Hand & Sword**
  Authors: Stephan Berwick and Ren Guangyi; foreword by Lou Reed. Description: The first book in English that dicusses the core links between the classical Chen Taijquan Old Frame First Road form and the Straightsword form. Photography by artist, Martin von Haselberg. www.truetaichi.com
- *The Way of the Bow: The Kyudo Path to a Disciplined Mind*
  Authors: Deborah Klens-Bigman and Raymond Sosnowski. Description: A discussion of some of the underlying principles in traditional Japanese archery with a detailed glossary. Publisher: Cliff Road Books. › www.barnesandnoble.com
- *The Way of Kata: A Comprehensive Guide to Deciphering Martial Applications*
  Authors: Lawrence A. Kane and Kris Wilder. Description: Even today, while the basic movements of kata are widely known, advanced practical applications and sophisticated techniques frequently remain hidden from the casual observer. The principles and rules for understanding kata are largely unknown. Publisher: YMAA Publication Center, Inc. › www.ymaa.com/publishing

## dvds

- **Advanced Practical Chin Na In Depth**
  Author: Dr. Yang, Jwing-Ming. Description: For your Chin Na to work in a real situation, you must master the technique so that it becomes an immediate natural reflex. This program focuses on interception, trapping and sealing the opponent, and keeping a sense of distance to avoid a counterattack. Publisher: YMAA Publication Center, Inc. › www.ymaa.com/publishing
- **The Basic-12 Curriculum Series**
  Author: Brian Johnson. Description: Geared toward those who wish to introduce Brazilian Jiu Jitsu into their existing curriculum, the *Basic 12 Curriculum* has all the essential positions, movements, and drilling methods you need to start your journey in BJJ today. Publisher: Moose Productions. › www.nwjja.com

- *Chen Taijiquan—Lao Jia Yi Lu & Straight Sword*
  Author: Ren, Guangyi. Description: In this DVD, Ren, Guangyi beautifully demonstrates two fundamental Chen-style taiji forms: the 75-movement long form, Lao Jia Yi Lu (Old Frame 1st Road), and the 49-movement straight sword form. Publisher: YMAA Publication Center, Inc. ‣ www.ymaa.com/publishing
- *Essential Techniques for MMA*
  Author: Tim Lajcik. Description: *Essential Techniques for* MMA, a five-DVD instructional series, integrates boxing and wrestling techniques into an effective mixed martial arts fighting system. Publisher: Martial Media Inc. ‣ www.TimLajcik.net
- *Kung Fu Body Conditioning: Traditional Training for Endurance and Power*
  Author: YMAA Retreat Center. Description: These traditional body-conditioning methods will gradually strengthen your bones, joints, and muscles, allowing you to develop speed, root, and explosive power without injury. Publisher: YMAA Publication Center, Inc. ‣ www.ymaa.com/publishing
- **MastersFromChina.com Video Productions**
  Description: Catalog of over 45 training DVDs with Chinese internal martial arts masters, including specialized understandings of Qigong, Taiji, Xingyi, Lanshou, Tongbei, Liuhebafa, Mind and Brain with George Xu, Susan Matthews, and many more. Publisher: Masters from China Video Productions. ‣ mastersfromchina.com
- *Primal Power: Unlocking the Body's Natural Grappling Abilities*
  Author: Kevin Secours. Description: 2-volume DVD set, to enhance understandings of the fundamental principles at the core of effective grappling. Publisher: Integrated Fighting Systems. ‣ www.montrealsystema.com
- *Sanchin Kata: Traditional Training for Karate Power*
  Author: Kris Wilder. Description: Sanchin Kata is known to develop extraordinary quickness and generate remarkable power. This program breaks down the form piece by piece, body part by body part, so that the hidden details of the kata are revealed. Publisher: YMAA Publication Center, Inc. ‣ www.ymaa.com/ publishing
- *Shaolin Long Fist Kung Fu: Advanced Sequences*
  Author: Nicholas C. Yang. Description: Taught and demonstrated by Nicholas Yang, each form is divided into four sections to help you learn gradually and proficiently. Both sequences are presented with in-depth instruction, training exercises, and martial applications. Publisher: YMAA Publication Center, Inc. ‣ www.ymaa.com/publishing
- *Simplified Tai Chi Chuan & Applications: 24 Postures and Standard 48 Postures*
  Author: Liang, Shou-Yu. Description: The popular "Simplified" 24-posture form is demonstrated by Master Liang with martial fighting applications. The form is shown from several angles, with breathing instructions. The Standard 48-posture form is also demonstrated. Publisher: YMAA Publication Center, Inc. ‣ www.ymaa.com/publishing

- *Tai Chi Energy Patterns*
  Author: Ramel Rones. Description: 6-hour, 2-DVD essential movements and training exercises. Learn to develop and utilize the internal (*qi*) energy that can be found within all Tai Chi movements. The energy circulation, mental visualizations, extensive breathing techniques, and physical skills taught for all Tai Chi styles. Publisher: YMAA Publication Center, Inc.
  ‣ www.ymaa.com/publishing
- **True Strength Yang DVD**
  Author: Stephan Berwick. Description: The author presents a systematic training method for strengthening and toughening the body with a body-hitting method inspired by he traditional Chinese systems of Tongbei, Fanzi, and PiKua. www.dragondoor.com
- **Uechi-Ryu Karate, Vol. 2: Building Blocks 2-DVDs**
  Author: Ihor Rymaruk. Review: "This DVD is a gold mine of practical information and is arguably the best instructional DVD available on Uechi-Ryu." Publisher: Iron Arm International. ‣ www.UechiRyu-Karate.com
- **Warhead: Russian Systema Combat Psychology**
  Author: Kevin Secours. Description: Outlines the role of psychological delivery mechanisms in self-defense scenarios. Publisher: Integrated Fighting Systems.
  ‣ www.montrealsystema.com
- *Wudang Taijiquan: Zhan-Zhuan, 108 Sequence and Martial Applications*
  Author: Taoist Monk Zhou, Xuan-Yun. Description: The complete 108-posture Wudang Taijiquan sequence is demonstrated, and each posture is instructed separately with martial applications. Each technique is taught and demonstrated in detail, making it easy for the viewer to learn. Publisher: YMAA Publication Center, Inc.
  ‣ www.ymaa.com/publishing

## supplies & services

- **American Buddhist Shim Gum Do Association**
  Description: Ongoing classes in sword, empty-hand forms (*shin boep*), self-defense (*ho shin sul*), long stick, monthly dharma talks, and offers a Korean Zen-based residential training program. ‣ www.shimgumdo.org
- **American Sambo Association**
  Description: Through classes, seminars, demonstrations, and cross-discipline affiliations, the American Sambo Association strives to introduce and educate the American public to the benefits of Sambo. ‣ www.ussambo.com
- **CAS Hanwei**
  Description: CAS Hanwei is the source for the finest reproduction arms and armor

for the martial artist and collector alike. Accept no substitute. ‣ www.cashanwei.com

- **East Coast Martial Art Supplies**
  Description: In business since 1979. Owned by Bob Elder. A brick-and-mortar store with lots of history. Specializing in traditional martial arts equipment.
  ‣ http://ecmas.info

- **EriksEdge.com**
  Description: Authentic antique swords and weapons for the martial artist and collector. Asia, Indonesia, the Philippines, Africa, and Oceania. ‣ EriksEdge.com

- **Gold Mountain Forge**
  Description: All our products are designed by Kinzan master swordsmith (David Goldberg) exclusively for Gold Mountain Forge. Martial-grade swords and items are fabricated in traditional (iron sand) *tamahagane*, and blades hand made entirely by Kinzan. Lifetime Guarantee. ‣ www.goldmountainforge.com

- **Mugendo Budogu LLC**
  Description: Provides the finest martial arts equipment available from Japan, including books, videos/DVDs, weapons, and clothing. ‣ www.budogu.com

- **Raven Studios**
  Description: Specializing in traditional Wing Chun wooden dummies and high-quality, hand crafted, hardwood training swords and weaponry for Chinese, Filipino, Japanese, Korean, and European martial arts. ‣ www.little-raven.com

- **SDKsupplies**
  Description: SDKsupplies.com is a supply company for a variety of high-quality martial arts equipment. Handmade and factory-sourced wooden weapons are our specialty. ‣ http://sdksupplies.netfirms.com

- **Shum Ying Jow Pai International Headquarters**
  Description: Headed by Grandmaster Leung Shum and Master Cecil A. Jordan, Shum Ying Jow Pai International Headquarters is the premier training facility for Northern Eagle Claw. ‣ www.yingjowpai.com

- **Skyjiro Forge**
  Description: Skyjiro Forge offers an excellent choice of blades, including swords made using traditional *oroshigane* (steel smelted from pure iron pieces), forge-folded, forged edge-tempered, and forged through-tempered blades. All our swords carry an international manufacturer's warranty. ‣ www.skyjiro.com

- **WoodenSwords.com – Purpleheart Armoury**
  Description: Wood sourced and manufactured in USA. Impact-grade hickory for the highest quality *bo*, *jo* and *hanbo* staves. Two- and three-layered lamination for improved strength and straightness. Also *dadao*, *bokken*, *naginata*, and *mokuju*.
  ‣ www.woodenswords.com

# index

academics and martial arts 10, 24, 26, 35
Adrogué, Manuel 40-43
*Aikido* (合氣道) xv
Alexander the Great 12
Alexio, Dennis 102
Amdur, Ellis 30
Anderson, Henk 63
animism 36
armbar 48, 49, 50
Armstrong, Hunter 28
arnis 13, 36, 82, 124-127
*Baguazhang* (八卦掌) 25, 53, 74-77
*Bajiquan* (八極拳) 140-143
Ball, David 86
Barakov, Alexander 94
Barton-Wright, E. W. 13
Bartitsu 13
Bates, Chris 74-75
*Billy Jack* (movie) 17
biomechanics 33
*bo* (staff) 111
Bodhidharma 3-4, 12
Bodiford, William 29
Boxer Rebellion 26
Boylan, Peter 44-47
Bradley, Sean 48-51
bridging 75
Brinkman, Marcus 74
Buddhism 12, 16, 25, 36
*bun bu ichi* (文武一) 2
Burroughs, Jake 52-57
*bushido* (武士道) 16
Cabales, Angel 78
cane 13, 124-127
Capoeira 13
Cartmell, Tim 52
Chambers, Quintin 28
Chandera, Edhi 63, 64
Chaudhuri, Joyotpaul 58-61
Chen, Panling (陳泮嶺) 74
Chen, Wangting (陳王庭) 66
Chen, Xiaowang (陳小旺) 66-68

Chen, Xiaoxing (陳小旺) 66
Chen, Zhaochi (陳照池) 66-67
Chenjiagou (陳家溝) 25, 66
Choi, Hong Hi (최홍희) 41
choke 82-83, 85
clinch 52-57
concussions, cerebral 34
Corcoran, John 15
cross punch 78-79, 81
Cunningham, Ray 38
Cunningham, Steve 144
Daoism 25
Davies, Phillip H. J. 62-65
DeMarco, Michael
   xiv-xvi, 2, 4-5, 8, 18, 30, 156-167
de Spa, Harry 62
DeRose, Dayn 94
diagonal flying 106-107, 109
Dillman, George 70, 73
Dohrenwend, Robert xv, 10-13
Donohue, John xiv, 2-9, 16
double-knives 136-139
Draeger, Donn 21, 28-31, 157-158
Duus, Eric 102
Farkas, Emil 15
Faulhaber, Carel 62-63
Fields, Aaron 94
Filipiak, Kai xv, 24-27
Five Ancestors Boxing (*Wuzuquan* 五祖拳) 63
Fong, Augustine (方致榮) 58
Fong, Leo 78-79
Fournet, Doug 94
fractures, bone 34-35
Friday, Karl 29
Fujian Crane Style 63
Fujian Tiger Style 63-65
Funakoshi, Ginchin (船越 義珍) 15
*Furyu* (magazine) 29
*Garuda Mas* (golden eagle) 63
Gaffney, David 66-69
Gauss, Chuck 124
Glover, Jesse 21

Goju-ryu (剛柔流) 98-101
Goshin Jutsu 144-146
Gracie, Helio 102
Grady, James xv, 14-17
grappling 100
Griffin, Mark 74
*Hapkido* (합기도) 48-51
Haruna, Matsuo 132
Hawaiian choke 82-83, 85
healing arts 20
Higginbotham, Will 70-73
Hinduism 36
Ho, Kamming (何金銘) 58
Hong, Tsehan (洪澤漢) 74-77
Hong, Yimian (洪懿棉) 74
Hong, Yixiang (洪懿祥) 30, 74
Hongji, Shaolin monk 148-149
hook punch 78-80
horse stance 141
Humphreys, Gregg 94
*iaido* (居合道) 44-47, 90-93
India 12, 38 159
Indonesia 36-37, 62, 159
Indonesian Pencak Silat Federation 37
injuries 33-35, 48
Ip, Man (Ip, Kaiman 葉繼問) 58
Islam 36
International Taekwon-Do Federation 41
James, Adam 78-81
Jay, Leon 70, 72, 82-85
Jay, Wally 82
Jeet Kune Do (截拳道) 21, 82
Ji Han-Jae (지한재) 48
Johnson, Charles 16
Jones, Llyr 86-89
judo (柔道) 10, 15, 44-47, 82,
    86-89, 102, 128-131, 144-147, 157
*Judo Illustrated* 28
jujutsu, jujitsu, jiujitsu (柔術)
    16, 70, 82, 102, 128-131, 144-147
Kalariplayattu xv, 38
Kano, Jigaro (嘉納 治五郎) 15

karate (空手) 10, 13, 15, 32-33,
    36, 41, 70, 98-101, 110-113, 157
kata (型/形) 70, 98-101
*katame-no-kata* (forms of control) 86-89
Kawachi, Ken 82
Keeley, Liam 28
Kernspecht, Keith 137
kick, axe 34
kick, roundhouse 34, 49, 51
Kimura, Masahiko (木村 政彦) 102
Kiyama, Hiroshi 44
Klens-Bigman, Deborah 90-93
kneebar 97
knife 118-123
Koepfer, Stephen 94-97
Korean Taekwondo Association 32
Kreiger, Pascal 28
Kudding, Richard 62
*Kung Fu* (T.V. series) 17
*kuntao* (拳道) 36-37, 62-65
*Kuntao Matjan* (Tiger Style) 62
Kurinnoy, Igor 94
*la canne* 13
Labbate, Marvin 98-101
Lajcik, Tim 102-105
Larkin, Tim 41
Lee, Bruce (Li, Xiaolong 李小龍)
    16-17, 21, 78, 82
legends 11, 18
Leung, Ting (Liang, Ting 梁挺) 136
Li, Shuwen (李書文) 140
Liem, Tjoei Kang (Lin, Cuigang 林粹剛) 63
Lin, Tangfang (林棠芳) 114-115
Liang, Xuexiang (梁學香) 114
Liu, Dechang 148
Liu, Yunqiao (劉雲樵) 140-141
Liu, Xiheng (劉錫亨) 106
Lo, Ban Teng (Lu, Wanding 盧萬定) 63
Lo, Benjamin Pang Jeng 106
locks 68, 84
    double-wrist lock 102-104
    finger lock 70, 72, 83

# index

hammerlock 70-72
shoulder lock 96
Lopez, Richard 38
Lowry, Dave xv, 28-31
Luo, Eric 74
Malaysia 36-37, 62
Malizewski, Michael xv, 18-23
Maniwa Nen-ryu (馬庭念流) 30
Mantis Boxing 52-53, 56-57, 114-117, 140
martial arts 25
Mason, Russ 16, 106-109
Mazek, George 124
McKenna, Mario 110-113
media and martial arts 14-17, 156-158
meditation 18, 20-23, 140
Meihua Tanglang Quan (梅花螳螂拳) 114-117
Miyagi, Chojun (宮城 長順) 11
military history 24
minorities 26
Minowa, Katsuhiko 110
Miyamoto, Musashi 132
mixed martial arts 18, 94, 102-105
monasteries 25, 26
Moo Duk Kwan (무덕관) 41
Moriya, Abi 74
movies 27
Muromoto, Wayne 29, 158
Musō Gonnosuke Katsuyoshi
 (夢想權之助勝吉) 132
Muso Shinden-ryu (夢想神伝流) 90-93
nage-no-kata (forms of throwing 投の形)
 86-89
Namitome, Shigenori 132
narratives 27
neck moping 56, 57
Netherlands 37
neutralizing 66-68, 108-109
Nihon Jujutsu (日本柔術) 128
Nihon Shoki (日本書紀) 15
Niten Ichi-ryu (二天一流) 131
noto (resheathing) 90-93
ogoshi (major hip throw 大腰) 45

Okazaki, Henry 82
Olympics 35, 102
osotogari (major outside reap 大外刈)
 128-130
Otani, Yoshiteru (大谷 芳照) 90
Pankration 12
parry 105
Pauka, Kirstin xv, 36-38
Pearlman, Steve 41
Pencak Silat, see silat
PERSILAT 37
Pieter, Willy xv, 32-35
Pittman, Allen 30
Plum Blossom Mantis Boxing 114-117
Presas, Remy 82, 124
Profatilov, Ilya 114-117
psychology 33
push-hands 67-68
Qi, Jiquan (戚繼光) 150
Qianzai Temple (千載寺) 149
qi, qigong (氣, 氣功) 22, 25, 140
randori-no-kata
 (free practice forms 乱取りの形) 86
Ratti, Oscar 7, 9, 29, 95, 165
Ray, Eugene 102
Reeders, Willem 38
reference sources 26
reiki (靈氣) 22
Relnick, Phil 28
roundhouse kick 48-49, 51
Ryukyu Kempo (琉球拳法) 70
Ryukyu kobudo (琉球古武道) 110-113
Sambo 13, 94-97, 118
sanchin (サンチン) kata 99
Sato, Shizuya 128
Savate 13
scarf hold 94-97
Schultz, Dave 102
Schultz, Mark 102
Secours, Kevin 118-123
secrets 10-11
Serrada Escrima 78

Servidio, Robert 38
Shaolin (少林) 3, 12, 25, 27, 148
Shi, Jingyan 148-149
Shindo Muso-ryu (神道夢想流) 13
Shinto Hatakage-ryu 44
Shinto Muso-ryu (神道夢想流) 44
Shinto-ryu (神道流) 132
Shinken, Taira (平 信賢) 110
Shotokan (松濤館) 10, 32, 41
Shuaijiao (Chinese wrestling 摔跤) 52-53, 56-57
shoulder strike (kao 靠) 143
silat 36-37, 62-65
silek 38
Sinmoo Hapkido (신무 합기도), see hapkido
Six Harmonies Praying Mantis 52-53, 56-57
Skoss, Diane 29
Skoss, Meik 28
Small Circle Jujitsu 70, 82-85
Smith, Ken 124-127
Smith, Robert W. 15, 21, 74, 106-107, 157, 165
spear 12, 140-141, 148-153
spirituality 18, 20-21
standing post practice 140
Star Wars (movie) 16
Su, Dongcheng (蘇東成) 74
Suino, Nicklaus 128-131
Svinth, Joseph 30
sweep 54-55
Systema 21, 118-123
Taekkyon (택견) 32
Taekwondo (태권도) 32-36, 40-43, 94, 141, 162
Taiji, Taijiquan (太極, 太極拳) 15, 22, 25, 36, 66-69, 74, 106-109
Taipiing Rebellion 27
takedown 52-57, 102
Taktarov, Oleg 94
taolu (practice routine 套路) 25
Taylor, Kim 132-135
tekko (tikko) 110-113

Thai boxing 36, 71
Thomas, Robert 86
Uchida, Ryugoro 13
Uchida-ryu Tanjojutsu (內田流短杖術) 13
Ueshiba, Morihei (植芝 盛平) 21-22
Vasiliev, Vladimir 21
Via Media Publishing 160-161
Vigney, Pierre 13
ving tsun, see yong chun
Wang, Maozhai (王茂齋) 149
Wang, Peisheng (王培生) 149
ward-off (peng 掤) 106-108
Washin-ryu (和真流) 144-145, 147
weaponry 12, 27, 110-113, 118-127, 136-141, 148-153
Webb, Jeff 136-139
Wei Kuen Do 78-81
Wing Chun, see Yong Chun
World Taekwondo Federation 32
Wright, Graham 86
Wu, Quanyou (吳全佑) 149
Wu Shu 148
wuxing (five-phase theory 五行) 140
Xingyiquan (形意拳) 52-55, 74
Yakimov, Igor 94
Yang, Chengfu (楊澄甫) 14, 106
Yang, Luchan (楊露禪) 149
Yang, Tony (Yang, Xiaodong 楊曉東) 140-143
Yiannakis, Andrew 144
Yiannakis, Linda 144-147
Yip, Man (葉問) 136
yoko garuma (modified side wheel 橫車) 128-129, 131
Yong Chun (詠春) 58-61, 136-139
Yoshimura, Hiroshi 110
Yu, Robert (Yu Lin-i) 74-75
Zhang, Yun (張雲) 148-153
Zhang, Zhunfeng (張峻峰) 74
Zheng, Manqing (鄭曼青) 15, 106-107

www.ingramcontent.com/pod-product-compliance
Lightning Source LLC
Chambersburg PA
CBHW041140110526
44590CB00027B/4079